THE
EDGE
OF THE
INSIDE

FRED SMITH

The Edge of the Inside

Library of Congress Cataloging-in-Publication Data
Fred Smith, 1946 –
The Edge of the Inside
1. Religion
2. Spirituality

ISBN 9798450599151

Cover design and text layout by Brad Wofford.

For more information on Fred Smith and his writings, please visit
www.thegathering.com.

Printed in the United States of America

DEDICATION

This book is dedicated to those whose example encouraged me to teach and, most important, persevere in teaching:
Louise Yelvington, Cecil Franklin, David Hubbard, and Lyle Schaller.

ACKNOWLEDGMENTS

I want to thank, first of all, my Sunday school classes over the years who have encouraged and supported me with great patience as a teacher. My family—especially my wife, Carol—has given up countless Saturdays for me to prepare. My gratitude to the churches and Bible studies that have allowed me great opportunities to teach and, finally, special thanks to copyeditor Amanda Varian who was able to take long and sometimes rambling lessons and edit them into a book.

CONTENTS

Introduction

Many years ago a friend asked me, "What do you think your best contribution will be? For what would you like to be remembered?" I did not need long to think about it. "I have been a Sunday school teacher for the largest part of my life now, and other than being a husband and father, I think that is the answer to your question. I am a Sunday school teacher."

Granted, it doesn't always feel that way when the alarm goes off at 5:00 every Sunday morning. That's when I put together the notes I've worked on all day Saturday. Some mornings it feels like a calling and other days more like a job. I suspect that is true for thousands of other teachers waking up early to prepare. We are not official ministers with a parish but there is something about the work—even when it feels most like a job—that carries the sense of being ordained to it.

Eugene Peterson said it well in describing the commitment of ordained pastors in congregations:

> This is not a temporary job assignment, but a way of life that we need lived out in our community. We know there will be days and months, maybe even years, when we won't feel like we are believing anything and won't want to hear it from you. And we know that there will be days and weeks and maybe even years when you won't feel like saying it. It doesn't matter. There may be times when we come to you as a committee or delegation and demand you tell us something else than what we are telling you now. Promise right now that you won't give in to what we demand of you.[1]

---

1   Eugene Peterson, *The Contemplative Pastor: Returning to the Art of Spiritual Direction* (Grand Rapids: Wm. B. Eerdmans Publishing, 1993), 139.

Scripture is full of instructions for teachers, but sometimes we need a short list about our work. We need a reminder of the essentials and especially in times of head-spinning change we must face up to new realities. It means starting with the question: "What is the world really like?" rather than the assumptions that made sense only a few years ago.

A teacher is not a harbor or an anchor, a sail or a rudder. We are keels. We help people manage in turbulent times by keeping them stable in the truth and in reality. In times of instability, people attach themselves to easy answers, sure things, strong leaders, institutions that promise security, heresies, novelties, cults, movements, extreme beliefs, or no beliefs at all.

One of the few items on the short list for me is found in Ephesians 4. We are to prepare people for maturity and works of service. The word *prepare* can mean several things. It describes mending nets, refitting a ship. or resetting a broken bone. It's not about making people perfect, and it assumes we've been through some wear and tear in our own lives.

Mending nets is constant. It's done after every use. It is daily and routine. Even tedious.

Refitting a ship is periodic. Barnacles accumulate. Wood decays. Holes are punched in the hull.

Resetting a bone is extreme and a once-in-a-lifetime thing for most people.

The work of a teacher in preparing people is all three:

- It is sitting around stitching—talking and working together.
- It is working with people in drydock and out of service for a time.
- It is standing by in the emergency room.

But it is not preparing people for being museum pieces or door prizes or merely pristine and pious. It is preparing them for works of service in a turbulent and changing world. A world that is going to bang them up, put dents in their hulls, tear their nets, and sometimes put them out of service for a time.

Richard Rohr wrote living on the edge of things is to be a doorkeeper and where a teacher serves best. "When you live on the edge of anything with respect and honor (and this is crucial!), you are in a very auspicious position. You are free from its central seductions. . . . When you are at the center of something, you usually confuse the essentials with the non-essentials, and get tied down by trivia, loyalty tests, and job security. Not much truth can happen there."[2]

The teacher, while not an insider, loves those on the inside even while they cannot be an insider. The teacher must remain on the edge of the inside. Rohr comments, "A doorkeeper must love both the inside and the outside of his or her group and know how to move between those two loves."

And that's what I think about every Sunday morning—moving between those two loves. That's my job and these are the people God has given me. So, yes, I do believe being a Sunday school teacher will be, for me, what has defined my life and I think this is true for so many of us in the "5:00 a.m. fellowship."

So, this book is not intended to be filled with brilliant insights into Scripture or to shake the roots of our beliefs. Instead, it is a selection of what I have promised to do from the start: to prepare people for works of service while living on the edge of the inside.

---

2   Richard Rohr's essay "On the Edge of the Inside: The Prophetic Position," https://cac.org/wp-content/uploads/2015/11/4-ON-THE-EDGE-OF-THE-INSIDE.pdf.

He who has learned in order to teach others,
while his own soul loathes instruction and wisdom,
will find that his lessons will be but mists of empty wind,
and showers of dust and earth upon the ground.

————————

Modern translation of *Shekel Hakodesh (The Holy Shekel)*
by Joseph Kimchi and Hermann Gollancz

I

THE SMALLEST THINGS

Text: Genesis 22

Two familiar stories of Abraham—found in Genesis 15 and Genesis 22—point to two different aspects of his faith. The first is in Genesis 15 where God appears to Abram (his name before God changed it) and responds to Abraham's question of inheritance. He is afraid he will die without an heir and everything will pass to a servant in his household—Eliezer of Damascus. We all know God's response. He showed him the stars in the sky and said, "'So shall your offspring be.' Abram believed the LORD, and he credited it to him as righteousness" (vv. 5–6). Abraham did nothing to show his faith. He simply believed.

The other story in Genesis 22 is not about the *origin* of the faith of Abraham. It is about the *test* of that faith and righteousness. As horrible as this test will be—"Take your son, your only son, whom you love—Isaac—and go to the region of Moriah. Sacrifice him there as a burnt offering on a mountain I will show you" (v. 2)—it is important not to see this as temptation or torture. There is a difference. A temptation is an attempt to take someone out of a relationship with God, and a test is to see how deep that relationship is. A temptation comes at the beginning of a process to lead someone to make bad choices. A test comes at the end of the process of teaching.

Abraham responds to God just as you would expect from someone who had learned to trust God over the course of his life. When God called him to pick up and move without any information about where he was going, he did that. His life had been one of following God into the unknown. So, when God calls him, Abraham responds with the word *heneni* ("I am yours to command"), which means: *You have my undivided attention and I am ready to do whatever you say even before I hear what it is.*

For us, that would have been an unbearable night, but there is nothing of that here in the passage. There is no dark night of the soul. No struggle. No crying out in protest. No anger or resentment. It is just silence and then obedience. It is an act of the will in the face of a conflict so great that only God can resolve it.

Had this been written today, the main emphasis would have been on Abraham's struggle. It would have been about Abraham and Isaac and how they deal with an impossible choice. But it's not.

Everything in me says this is wrong, and yet I know the voice of God.

Abraham could not know the outcome of his obedience, but he knew it was necessary. In the same way, our obedience is not just about us—but about generations to come. Things that we cannot see are affected by the smallest acts of obedience on our part.

"He looked up and saw the place in the distance" (v. 4). In a sense, that is the mark of Abraham's life. He could always see in the distance in spite of the present circumstances. He could see what no one else saw. That's how he is described in Hebrews 8:8, isn't it? "By faith Abraham, when called to go to a place he would later receive as his inheritance, obeyed anyway, even though he did not know where he was going." He welcomed the future from a distance. "He was looking forward to the city with foundations, whose architect and builder is God" (8:10).

Abraham looked through the present all the way to the unimaginable. What does he say to his servants in Genesis 22:5? "WE will worship and then WE will come back to you" (emphasis mine). In spite of the seeming inevitability of the death of his son and his future and the promise of God, he saw something he could never have explained to the servants. What does it say in Hebrews 11:19? "Abraham reasoned that God could even raise the dead . . ." Some of us can see through a window, some through a veil, but Abraham saw through a brick wall!

What Paul and the book of Hebrews are saying about Abraham is NOT that Abraham believed God would spare his son but Abraham believed God would raise the dead. That's a huge difference. Yes, we'll see that God spared the son (Gen. 22:12), but that was not in Abraham's mind. There was only one answer possible—the same God who could take life could give it back. He expected Isaac to die but he was not without hope. The pressure of an impossible situation reveals an impossible solution.

Each of us has a different test in life, played out in different ways. But the basis is always the same. What is the one thing in life you trust more than any other?

Here are four things to consider in our own lives:

1. **Are we willing to obey in the smallest things, or are we waiting for the grand moment?** God is not interested in heroics or in our choosing to be martyrs. He gives us daily quizzes of obedience. Have we been kind? Have we been trustworthy? Have we been a sign that points others to God? Those are what build character over many years.

2. **Is God calling us to let go of a blessing? We want to hold on, don't we?** I think Abraham was willing to start from zero again. It's one thing to lose it all but quite another to think of God taking it all away intentionally. But as my father used to say, "Stay loose to things." This means understanding what Paul means by being content no matter what—whether little or much (Phil. 4:11–12).

3. **Are we open to trusting God even though we do not see, or are we more like Sarah who laughed because God's promise defied her experience?** Notice that Sarah was not consulted before Abraham set off that morning with the two servants and Isaac. She would have argued him out of it just as she did when she made him believe God

was never going to give him an heir through her but through Hagar. There are times to get counsel and advice, and then there are times to act alone. There are times when common sense is not the same thing as the reason of God.

4. **If you glibly ask to see God, are you prepared for the consequences?** Seeing God exacts an awful price. Seeing God means you are drawn into the suffering as well as the joy. Faith is tested and great faith is tested greatly. We want the experience of glory but not the sharing in his sufferings. We want a little peek into the majesty of God but without our lives being affected in ways we would not choose.

Faith is believing the promise if only from a distance. It is lived out by those who are content to live as aliens and strangers on earth knowing that there is a better country which God has prepared, and that we can be certain of what we do not see.

2

BURY MY HEART

Text: Genesis 29–30

Weddings are typically beautiful events with the music, candles, glamorous bride, and handsome groom. The festive receptions—with delectable food and joyful laughter—completes the picture. That does not describe this wedding. In fact, had there been the ritual invitation for someone to stand up and object, this would have been the time.

Certainly, it was love at first sight for Jacob and Rachel. "When Jacob saw Rachel daughter of Laban, his mother's brother, and Laban's sheep, he went over and rolled the stone away from the mouth of the well and watered his uncle's sheep. Then Jacob kissed Rachel and began to weep aloud" (Gen. 29:10–11). Yes, we call that kissing cousins. It was not only romantic but also a sign of belonging to the same family. It was important back then to preserve the family line, wealth, traditions, and values. But this union would present unusual problems from the very beginning.

First, Jacob totally ignored the traditions of his new home. The youngest daughter was not supposed to marry before the eldest. Second, the unhealthy combination of the two dysfunctional families was obvious.

You could start with Jacob's uncle, Laban. He was a character study in duplicity, greed, and double-dealing. The family was full of manipulation and deceit. Both sisters—Rachel and Leah—were named for and worked in the family business. Rachel means "sheep" and Leah means "cow." Laban was serious about his work! In Texas that would be like a man in the petroleum business naming his daughters Oil and Gas.

Jacob's family is much the same—favoritism, deceit, envy, jealousy, uncontrollable anger, rivalry, and theft.

And then marriage brings the cousins together.

Deception began early as the sisters are switched on the honeymoon, and the first words we hear from Jacob after the wedding are not "You are my beloved" but "What have you done to me?"

Not a great start. Leah knows she is the pawn in the game and unloved. She's the placeholder until Jacob can have the one he really wants and Laban can get the upper hand.

But Jacob agrees to work seven more years to have Rachel. Laban knows Jacob is on a short fuse, so he is married to Leah for only one week until Laban gives Rachel to Jacob to be his second wife.

It is worse than any reality show with the sisters using children, Jacob, and the handmaidens as weapons in their contest with each other over Jacob and their place in the pecking order. Beautiful Rachel is reduced to screaming at Jacob: "When Rachel saw that she was not bearing Jacob any children, she became jealous of her sister. So, she said to Jacob, 'Give me children, or I'll die!' Jacob became angry with her and said, 'Am I in the place of God, who has kept you from having children?'" (Gen. 30:1–2).

That had to feel like a knife in the heart to Rachel. *God has kept you from having children.*

Leah has found something she can do better than Rachel: she can have children one after the other. But look at the sadness of Leah's life reflected in the meaning of her children's names:

Reuben – Surely my husband will love me now
Simeon – The Lord heard I am not loved
Levi – My husband will become attached to me

Every child was a reminder to Leah and the entire family that she was unloved, unwanted, and undesired by her husband.

But something happens along the way in the middle of the child wars. Leah names her fourth son Judah. "This time I will praise the LORD." It can also be translated as "God will lead." It was not about her relationship with Jacob or the pain in her life. It was an expression of trust and the birth of trust in her life.

The rivalry with Rachel remains, but something has changed in Leah's life: she realizes that God will lead. She is no longer the victim.

Our prayer so often is that God would change our circumstances first, and when he does not, we give up or become bitter. The psychotherapist and Holocaust survivor Viktor Frankl wrote:

> We who lived in concentration camps can remember the men who walked through the huts comforting others, giving away their last piece of bread. They may have been few in number, but they offer sufficient proof that everything can be taken from a man but one thing: the last of the human freedoms—to choose one's attitude in any given set of circumstances, to choose one's own way.[3]

Long before Frankl wrote that, Leah experienced it.

And then, we hear almost nothing more about Leah. Rachel finally has a child, Joseph, and then dies having her second, Benjamin. Jacob buries her

---

3   Viktor Frankl, *Man's Search for Meaning* (1959; repr. Boston, MA: Beacon Press, 2006), 65–66.

on the way to Bethlehem and puts up a stone pillar by her tomb. Then he moves on.

It's almost one hundred years until Leah's name is mentioned again—at Jacob's death in Egypt—and it is nearly a footnote unless you read it carefully:

> "Bury me with my fathers in the cave in the field of Ephron the Hittite, the cave in the field of Machpelah, near Mamre in Canaan, which Abraham bought along with the field as a burial place from Ephron the Hittite. There Abraham and his wife Sarah were buried, there Isaac and his wife Rebekah were buried, and there I buried Leah." (Gen. 49:29–31)

In other words, *bury me with Leah.*

What a remarkable change from their first encounter and their first years together.

"You've tricked me with this weak-eyed cow" has turned to "I want to be next to her forever."

What is the end result of the silent years in Jacob's life with Leah?

All the brothers and their families are together—all seventy of them—brought there to Egypt by Rachel's son, Joseph. They are at peace. There is no more manipulation, jealousy, or anger. They have become a family in spite of all their differences.

This is the remarkable story of a woman who outgrew her circumstances, her handicap, the unfairness of her life, and silently affected one of the most difficult men in Scripture and generations coming afterward.

But there is one more thing . . . because, ultimately, it is from *Leah's* line—Judah—that Jesus is born! It is from the son named "God Will Lead." Isaiah describes him like this:

"He had no beauty or majesty to attract us to him, nothing in his appearance that we should desire him. He was despised and rejected by mankind, a man of suffering . . ." (Isa. 53:2–3)

Sound familiar?

But what a difference has been made by the descendant of the one who was not wanted . . . He is the long-expected Messiah—the joy of man's desiring—Jesus.

3

I WILL BE WITH YOU

Text: Genesis 31

When we are in the middle of a struggle, it is difficult to see its purpose. We simply want a way out. It's often tempting to bail, but then, later in life, we find it is those very difficulties that shaped us and our character.

Jacob spent twenty years of working in difficult circumstances for his father-in-law, Laban, bringing success to his estate with no recognition, and then goes out on his own by leaving Laban.

If there is one thread that is consistent in the life of Jacob it is this: "I will be with you." At every point of change in his life, he hears that from God. Jacob may not know where he is going or what he is going to do, but there is always the affirmation from God that he is not completely alone.

Not many people have that assurance in their lives—or perhaps not many people realize it. They have come to believe they are on their own so they are afraid of change or risk. They are unable to trust that God is with them when difficulties or even new opportunities come. Their circumstances determine their faith.

God does not promise us a charmed life with no obstacles or hardships. If you look at the lives of the saints, you will often see one theme—difficulty. It may be physical, emotional, or spiritual. They have learned that the pursuit of maturity is not the pursuit of happiness. Instead, it is through the road of trials and even suffering.

This was certainly true in the life of Jacob. He came to Laban's home looking for refuge and a wife. Instead, what did he find? Infighting, jealousy, envy, and being treated unfairly by his in-laws. Jacob confronts Laban,

> "I have been with you for twenty years now. Your sheep and goats have not miscarried, nor have I eaten rams from your flocks. I did not bring you animals torn by wild beasts; I bore the loss myself. And you demanded payment from me for whatever was stolen by day or night. This was my situation: The heat consumed me in the daytime and the cold at night, and sleep fled from my eyes. It was like this for the twenty years I was in your household. I worked for you fourteen years for your two daughters and six years for your flocks, and you changed my wages ten times." (Gen. 31:38–41)

But Jacob perseveres and makes the best of a bad situation and is not constantly asking for signs or signals from God about when things are going to get better. Some of us want constant inspiration, affirmation, and encouragement—we cannot survive the "in-between times."

As hard as it is for us as parents to see our children go through difficulties early in life, we cannot help them by removing challenges that can build character and perseverance. Writer John Gardner said, "History never looks like history when you are living through it." The same is true for those parts of our life that are the building blocks of future success. We want the pursuit of happiness and not the pursuit of character.

There is almost always a price to success—and often the price is the loss or change of relationships. My father struggled with one of his brothers their whole lives because Dad's success only made his brother more and more resentful of him. In the end, his brother died a bitter man isolated not only from his parents and other brothers, but from his own wife and children. Instead of being proud of his brother, his resentment destroyed his life.

After twenty years of God's silence and Jacob playing the hand he is dealt, he hears from God that it is time to leave. Even Laban's daughters recognize what has happened. "Do we still have any share in the inheritance of our father's estate? Does he not regard us as foreigners? Not only has he sold us, but he has used up what was paid for us. Surely all the wealth that God took away from our father belongs to us and our children. So do whatever God has told you" (31:14–16). Feeling robbed by their father, they are ready to leave as well. Finally—they can all agree on something!

This is where the story takes a permanent turn in the life of Jacob.

Rachel responds to being treated unfairly by stealing her father's household gods on the way out. It's a puzzling story, as we're not altogether sure about why she did it. She could have wanted something to remind her of home, or to keep her father from worshiping false gods. Maybe it was a sign of her total transfer of loyalty from her father to Jacob. I believe it had something to do with it being the one thing she could do in leaving that would hurt him the most. "If I cannot have what is rightfully mine, then I will even the score and take what is yours."

How does Laban respond to everyone leaving? "What have you done? You've deceived me, and you've carried off my daughters like captives in war. . . . You have done a foolish thing. . . . The women are my daughters, the children are my children, and the flocks are my flocks. All you see is mine" (vv. 26–28, 43).

Though Jacob is angry about the twenty years he has served Laban and received nothing but resentment and no appreciation, he also recognizes that it is God who has protected him and made him a success. He does not claim it as his own doing. "If the God of my father, the God of Abraham and . . . Isaac, had not been with me, you would surely have sent me away empty-handed. But God has seen my hardship and the toil of my hands" (v. 42). It is not pride speaking. It is the recognition that what he has comes from God. Jacob has matured through difficulties. He now sees the protection of God in his life without becoming prideful.

Jacob never works for anyone else ever again. He and Laban come to an agreement they will leave each other alone, and that is the last we hear of Laban and his family. My guess is nothing much changes for them and they likely continue to fight among themselves about who owns everything.

It does not mean that Jacob's family is free of the same envy and jealousy. We'll see that later in the story of Joseph, his brothers, and the coat of many colors. But Jacob moves on—a better, wealthier, and wiser man than he was twenty years ago.

4

GOOD BONES

Text: Genesis 49

Dying was discussed differently in the Old Testament. People talked about being "gathered to my fathers," which meant even in death you were a part of a larger family. You were taught your whole life that even in death you had certain responsibilities toward the family that remained—especially if you were the head of the family. You prepared for it. You didn't avoid it.

In our world today, the crunch between technology and communication to the patient is most apparent at the end of life. One oncologist said, "Intangible things get lost, like talking to patients." Everyone is caught in a web of conflicting expectations and not knowing how to deal with it. But that was not true in Jacob's time. The head of the family had spent many hours thinking about the future of his children and the blessing he would give. These were handcrafted after years of observation and consideration.

The blessing was not always pleasant and it wasn't always a final "I love you." It could be harsh or encouraging. It could be long or short. Look at the several blessings in Genesis 49: "Reuben . . . you will no longer excel. . . . Simeon and Levi . . . I will scatter them in Jacob and disperse them in Israel. . . . Issachar is a rawboned donkey" (vv. 4–5, 14). Try to imagine living with *that* as your father's last words to you.

But then there were other blessings: "The scepter will not depart from Judah, nor the ruler's staff from between his feet, until he to whom it belongs shall come and the obedience of the nations shall be his. . . . Dan will provide justice for his people. . . . Asher's food will be rich" (vv. 10, 16, 20).

And then we come to Joseph's blessing—the favorite child:

> "Joseph is a fruitful vine,
> a fruitful vine near a spring,
> whose branches climb over a wall.
> With bitterness archers attacked him;
> they shot at him with hostility.
> But his bow remained steady,
> his strong arms stayed limber,
> because of the hand of the Mighty One of Jacob,
> because of the Shepherd, the Rock of Israel,
> because of your father's God, who helps you,
> because of the Almighty, who blesses you
> with blessings of the skies above,
> blessings of the deep springs below,
> blessings of the breast and womb.
> Your father's blessings are greater
> than the blessings of the ancient mountains,
> than the bounty of the age-old hills.
> Let all these rest on the head of Joseph,
> on the brow of the prince among his brothers."

These have been the themes of Joseph's life. Fruitfulness. Overcoming obstacles. Steadiness. A prince among his brothers.

The word *inheritance* comes from a word that originally meant "assignment"—not merely gift. This is Joseph's inheritance—and responsibility for the balance of his life. In spite of his brothers' conniving, hostility, jealousy, fear, dependence, and resentment, Joseph is *among them*.

After Jacob's death—seventeen years after coming to Egypt—it's clear not much has changed with the brothers.

When Joseph's brothers saw that their father was dead, they said, "What if Joseph holds a grudge against us and pays us back for all the wrongs we did to him?" So they sent word to Joseph, saying, "Your father left these instructions before he died: 'This is what you are to say to Joseph: I ask you to forgive your brothers the sins and the wrongs they committed in treating you so badly.' Now please forgive the sins of the servants of the God of your father." When their message came to him, Joseph wept. His brothers then came and threw themselves down before him. "We are your slaves," they said (Gen. 50:15–18).

Of course, they have always been his slaves in the sense that their lives have been controlled by their hatred, resentment, and fear of him. That's what happens when the measure of your life is reacting to someone else or comparing yourself to them. You never live your own life because you are a slave to whatever keeps you tied to them.

But Joseph's response to his brothers is as clear a picture of God's love as any in the Old Testament. He is not cynical, angry, or hardened. In fact, Joseph weeps more than anyone else in the Old Testament—six times! He is overcome with joy, grief, sorrow, and gratitude.

- He is constantly reassuring them.
- He provides for them. He settles them and gives them work that is productive.
- He speaks kindly to them.
- Even when they betray him, he is kind to them.
- He is constant and steady.

In spite of our being too often like the brothers, God's love for us is the same—unchangeable and fixed, forever and everlasting. I think for most of us that is the biggest obstacle in our lives—knowing for certain that we are loved by God.

Bones are what holds us together. I've thought about what held Joseph's life together and how we can learn from the "bones" of his life.

1. Responsibility was the theme of his life. He took his duties and

opportunities seriously no matter the circumstances.

2. He valued relationships of commitment and respect. When Potiphar's wife tried to seduce Joseph, he would not give in out of respect for Potiphar and for God. Then, in spite of their mistreatment of him, Joseph takes care of his brothers to the end of his life.

3. He rested in God's purpose for his life. He did not panic. After Jacob's death, Joseph says to his brothers, "You intended to harm me, but God intended it for good to accomplish what is now being done, the saving of many lives" (Gen. 50:20). The word *(cashab)* used to describe the brothers' conniving and conspiring is the same word for "weaving." In other words, God wove their conspiracy for evil into the fabric of Joseph's life.

4. Finally, he was in control of his ego because he and everyone around him understood his success came from God.

Even in death many years later, Joseph stays "among his brothers." For four hundred years Joseph's bones remain in Egypt until they are taken with Moses and Joshua back to Canaan. The bones of Joseph were more than a shrine or a relic for the people during their hard years in Egypt. They became a symbol of hope and looking forward to deliverance. They were not only a reminder of better times in the past but an assurance that God, while silent, had not abandoned them.

Responsibility, integrity, commitment, respect, resting in God's purpose for your life; realizing God's gifts and making use of them—these are good bones to build your life on and to leave behind.

5

BASKET CASE

Text: Exodus 2

We all love a good story. Neuroscientists even say that our brain is wired to respond to stories because they have a pattern that is easy to grasp. When I say "story" I don't mean to say it is fiction. No, it simply means it is the truth written in a particular form that makes it even more memorable for us. It gets beneath our radar. So it is with the story of Moses.

This is the most important birth story in the Old Testament—in a sense, the birth of the Old Testament savior. Without Moses there would not be a Jewish nation. There was a Jewish people because of Abraham but not a Jewish nation with a founding document—the Ten Commandments.

Let's set the scene of Moses' story with examining the fear and foolishness of the villain: Pharaoh. There is fear because of his power and his edict to destroy every male child, but the real point is how clever the Jewish women and midwives are. He is powerful but stupid. He is capable of making them slaves, but it is out of fear of their abilities. How often this is true in Jewish history. Their traditions are filled with stories about outwitting tyrants—think about Esther. Tyrants are real but temporary and, in the end, foils for God.

All of us have Pharaohs in our lives. It may be someone on the outside who appears to have power over us. In that case, we want to hold on to what is at risk for as long as we can and not let go. After all, we are protecting something precious. Or it may be a Pharaoh on the inside who is fearful of others. We are always on guard against people who intimidate us or are unfamiliar to us or we assume everyone not a slave to our ideas must be an enemy.

Another point to notice is the initial lack of names for any of the main characters in Exodus 2: Pharaoh; Moses' mother, father, and sister; the servants and the princess; even the baby has no name. After three months his mother has not named him.

It's not like they are anonymous; it is more like everyone at this point in the story are shadow figures or props on the stage. The focus of the entire story is really the naming of Moses. Everyone else is there to lead us to that.

Eventually, we do discover the names of his parents (Exod. 6:20). And, like many names in Scripture, they have a particular meaning. The mother's name is Jochebed which means "the glory of God," and the father is Amram which means "an exalted people." In a sense, their names are fulfilled through their son—even while for a time they remain nameless and off to the side.

I think about that with my own children. Often our role for a time is to be nameless and unnoticed, but then later we find out that our purpose is fulfilled through their lives in ways we could not predict. Sometimes we, like Moses' parents, are only revealed later in their lives and we have to fight the temptation to claim credit or to want recognition. God is a God of generations, and it is not our purpose to always look for significance in our lifetime. What we do may not receive any recognition, but at some point our purpose will be fulfilled.

It is interesting to note the word for *baskets* throughout Scripture. The same word is used five times:

1. the ark of Noah (Gen. 6:14)

2. the story of Moses (Exod. 2:3)

3. the ark of the covenant (Exod. 37:1)

4. the story of Jesus feeding the 5,000 after the death of John (Luke 9:17)

5. the way in which Paul was rescued from certain death in Damascus (Acts 9:25)

There is a consistent theme each time we see an ark or a basket—they come at the end of something and a new beginning.

1. Noah – The end of one world and the beginning of another.

2. Moses – The end of bondage and the beginning of a new nation.

3. Ark of the covenant – The end of the gods of Egypt and the beginning of the presence of God.

4. Feeding the 5,000 – The end of the ministry of John the Baptist and the beginning of a new chapter in the ministry of Jesus.

5. Paul in Damascus – The end of his life as a persecutor and the beginning of his ministry to the Gentile world.

God's "basket cases" are reserved for special times. Whenever you see a basket, you know something unusual is happening.

What I find to be most remarkable in this story is his mother. She knew even at three months old that he was special: "At that time Moses was born, and he was no ordinary child. For three months he was cared for by his family" (Acts 17:20).

How did they know that? There was no appearance of an angel—no indication there was anything extraordinary about this child, and yet I have to believe that his mother knew it. And that is what makes what she did even more powerful. She turned loose of what was most precious to her at the time when the child needed her the most. She did not abandon him or abdicate, but she carefully built a boat and released him. There was no word from the Lord to Jochebed like Abraham. It was absolute faith and belief that God's ultimate purpose for her child was more at risk by her keeping him than letting him go.

But look how the child comes back to her. There would be no way to engineer such a thing (see Exod. 2:7–9). The difference is important. She is now the child's nurse but not his mother. She has to give up any claim to the child that was hers by right in order for the child to live. Not only that, but she gives him up *twice*—once at three months and then again when he is older.

Of course, there is more to this than a history of Moses, isn't there? This story has been a guide to me for years because I can see myself in both Pharaoh and the mother! What about you?

- Are there Pharaohs in your life that are making you hold on to something and think *This cannot live without me*?
  It may be a child or a relationship. It may be an organization for which you feel responsibility. It may be a dream. I don't know what it is, but there is a time to release what is most precious.

- Are you feeling nameless?
  I think "making a name for ourselves" is one of our greatest temptations (see Genesis 11 with the Tower of Babel).

- Are you ready for a basket?
  To let go of what you think needs hiding.
  To make an ending and a new beginning.
  To say good-bye to your role.
  To put something in the boat and push it out.
  To let go of what has a purpose larger than you understand at the moment.

I better understand the hymn "I Surrender All" through this story of Moses. There are times in life when that is exactly what is required—what is surrendered in faith becomes what it was intended to be all along.

6

PASS IT ON

Text: Joshua 23–24

"Now I am about to go the way of all the earth . . ."

Sounds like a dramatic yet poetic way to announce one's death, doesn't it? That is exactly what Joshua does in chapter 23. He has done what God instructed and, like Moses, he has concerns about their future. Yet, he does not leave any centralized structure in place. Joshua is not building a nation but a family of tribes, each with their own inheritance. God gives them a covenant. It's the riskiest arrangement possible. Nothing but local leadership—no Moses or Joshua to lead them now. No successor. Only one thing could keep them together—obedience.

Joshua assembles the people in Shechem, reinforcing their sense of history and calling.

- Shechem is where God first appeared to Abraham and made the first promise in Genesis 12. "To your offspring I will give this land" (v. 7).

- Shechem is where Jacob settled after leaving Laban and meeting Esau. It is where he dug the well we read about in John 4—the story of Jesus and the woman at the well.

- Shechem is where Jacob calls on his household to get rid of the foreign gods. "So they gave Jacob all the foreign gods they had . . . and Jacob buried them under the oak at Shechem" (Gen. 35:4).

Shechem is "hallowed ground" and the symbolic center of their story. It is the site of turning points in their lives where God was revealed, recommitments were made, and legacies were established. Everything they believe about their relationship with God started here. This is the core of their identity.

Joshua wants the tribes of Israel to choose. He gives them two options: serve God or serve other gods (Josh. 24:15). The options are just as limited today, but no one likes that.

Today one side says, "You are free to choose but not free from serving. You are not a free agent. You cannot be objective or agnostic or non-aligned. You do not have unlimited choices and you cannot cobble together your own version of religion."

While another side replies, "I don't have to choose one or the other. It's not like Republican or Democrat are the only choices now. You cannot limit me that way. I'll abstain. I'll wait until I see something I like. I don't like being pressured to make an irrevocable choice."

There are different degrees of choices:

- Picking one peach out of a hundred good ones is difficult but not life changing.
- Choosing one of two careers is important but not fatal.
- Choosing a spouse is life changing.
- Choosing between obedience and fidelity to God and slavery to other gods is the most important decision in life. It defines us and determines everything else we do.

But the tribes agree too quickly, and Joshua pushes back at them: "You are not able to serve the LORD. He is a holy God" (v. 19). In other words, "Don't take this lightly. Understand the consequences of what you are doing before making this covenant. Once you do this, you are agreeing to live in a certain way with restrictions and limitations and responsibilities."

We have no record of Joshua's family. There is never any mention of a wife or children. He is part of the tribe of Ephraim and the son of Nun, but that is all we know. It's ironic that his famous declaration in verse 15—"As for me and my household, we will serve the LORD"—has become the most popular Christian door sign for the home, because the word *oikos* means so much more than just our family. "Household" was a word for all the relationships in our lives—inside and outside the home. Today, we would call it "circles of influence." It means we will serve the Lord and live with integrity not just at home. It means we will think of ourselves as responsible to represent God not just to our children but especially with people we influence.

In Judges chapter 2 we find out what happens next: "After Joshua had dismissed the Israelites, they went to take possession of the land, each to his own inheritance. The people served the LORD throughout the lifetime of Joshua and of the elders who outlived him and who had seen all the great things the LORD had done for Israel. . . . After that whole generation had been gathered to their ancestors, another generation grew up who knew neither the LORD nor what he had done for Israel" (vv. 6–7, 10).

Wait . . . what? How could they not know the Lord or what he had done for Israel?

It sounds like the elders made some assumptions about passing on beliefs that were wrong. They did not have a training program. They had worship, festivals, ordinances, and activities, but they did not pass on the relationship with God or the understanding of the covenant. They stopped remembering with their children.

I remember the old Training Union when I was young. It was held the hour before the evening service in thousands of Baptist churches and we were taught doctrine, history, what we believed, and Christian principles—and thousands of kids suffered through it. It faded away long before the evening service did. It took time and the whole family had to do it. Unless you are intentional about training people—especially the young—in what they believe, they will not believe it in the next generation.

Beginning in the 1930s, a praiseworthy goal of adapting the Christian faith to appeal to the young occurred, which revitalized American Christianity. A drawback has been the juvenilization of Christianity—the process by which the beliefs, practices, and developmental characteristics of adolescents become accepted as appropriate for adults. This has sometimes ended with both youth and adults embracing immature versions of the faith.

Informal church services, while effective at reaching the unchurched, often create an environment that does not foster long-term growth of discipleship: If you ask the people why they go to church or what they value about their faith, they'll say something like, "Having faith helps me deal with my problems." Juvenilization happened when no one was looking. In the first stage, Christian youth leaders created youth-friendly versions of the faith in a desperate attempt to save the world. Some hoped to reform their churches by influencing the next generation. In the second stage, a new American adulthood emerged that looked a lot like the old adolescence. Fewer and fewer people outgrew the adolescent Christian spiritualities they had learned in youth groups; instead, churches began to cater to them.

We are so focused on the future and innovation that we consider our traditions as limiting and uninteresting. We want to renegotiate our choices and kick the can down the road on our consequences, or we want someone who will protect us those consequences. That is not the message of Joshua. We cannot choose *not* to choose—and in the end, we make a choice about whom we serve and about restraints we impose on ourselves. Life or death. Fidelity or unfaithfulness.

7

THE SUCCESS TRAP

Text: Judges 1–2

One of the major obstacles to the ratification of our Constitution was the disagreement over the power of the Executive Branch to make decisions that affected the individual states. It was the same for Israel. There was a succession of heroes like Moses, the liberator; Joshua the military leader for conquering the Promised Land; and the Judges when they were needed to unite the people. However, there was never any intention to have single leaders after that. Everything was to be organized by tribes and local government. No President. No King. It would be like our having states but no national government.

God told the Israelites several times in Exodus 23:30 and Joshua 13:6 that he and the people would drive out the Canaanites from the land. Some tribes do better than others at driving out the Canaanites. Some have to cooperate with each other and some do it on their own. Some few are unsuccessful and live with the consequences. There is no attempt to form a national effort to drive out the Canaanites.

The assumption is every tribe is capable of governing itself because they all have the same set of values in the Law. Such a system assumes people have the ability to govern themselves and do not need external controls except in extreme circumstances. Unfortunately, they *did* need external controls. God put them in the middle of an almost impossible test. Canaan was a land of vile practices—a cesspool of temptation for Israel. You might say there was no worse place God could have put them. Everything in it appealed to their worst natures. But God did not command them to clean up the Canaanites. He told them to drive them out of the land completely because they had violated the land itself with their corruption. He needed them to fumigate—not use air freshener.

The tribes drove out some, and thought reducing others to slaves was adequate. But they left their gods and their altars intact. They did not understand the corrupting power of what they had let remain. That's always the case when we compromise. We think we are getting a good deal or the best of both worlds. The Canaanites said to them, "Let us stay and work for you." But what the Israelites discovered is the very same thing that had enslaved the minds of the Canaanites would enslave them as well. They soon lost their ability to resist and were, as God promised, ensnared by the gods of the Canaanites: "They will become traps for you, and their gods will become snares to you" (Judg. 2:3).

A snare is a very particular thing. It is not like a minefield. A minefield is simply hidden destruction. A snare is not an overwhelming force; it depends on the nature of the prey as much as the design of the snare. That is what evil understands so well. False gods are not content merely to trick or make us stumble. The purpose of a snare is to catch an animal to kill it and eat it. False gods are not just false; they are fatal. Evil is not content to fool us; it desires us.

> Each person is tempted when they are dragged away by their own evil desire and enticed. Then, after desire has conceived, it gives birth to sin; and sin, when it is full-grown, gives birth to death. (James 1:14–15)

Desires are typically not overtly evil. We don't get up in the morning with the thought of doing something evil on our list. In fact, they are mostly distortions of good things we have allowed to get out of place. St. Augustine called them "disordered loves"—love out of order. Augustine helps us see there is an order to love. He said we should love God, love others, and then love ourselves.

A desire may be for something good, but instead of waiting for the object of that desire—for joy, peace, contentment, love—we settle for a weak substitute instead. We choose happiness over joy, certainty over peace, and excitement over love. And we are dragged away by these cheap imitations and end up in sin because we have allowed a short-cut to drag us off the path. This is why they are called fruit of the spirit. They are what we should desire but they take time to ripen.

The Israelites wept aloud and offered sacrifices (Judg. 2:4–5), but they did change their behavior. Nothing hardens the heart like frequent and sometimes extravagant sorrow with no change in behavior. Mere sorrow is not what God desires. It is a change in our behavior. It is a redirection of desire. We have three stories of heroes here at the beginning and at the end of each that comment that the people were at peace as long as the hero lived—up to eighty years of good behavior—and then they revert to their faithless ways. There is no law in their hearts. They cannot master themselves. They do what is right in their own eyes. They were, at least at the beginning, attempting to do what made sense to them. These gods made crops grow. These gods made women have children. These gods made life easier. These gods were not evil. They were just another way to what God had in mind for us anyway.

The irony, of course, is that in the end they have no common understanding of what is right. The society disintegrates into small factions because "in those days everyone did what was right in his own eyes" (Judg. 21:25 ESV). It was the first postmodern society. What is right for you may not be right for me. Who is to say? What is right is whoever has the most votes.

In C. S. Lewis's *The Screwtape Letters*, senior demon Screwtape instructs his nephew Wormwood just how easy it is to ensnare humans and keep them from God, to whom they refer as the Enemy:

> But do remember, the only thing that matters is the extent to which you separate the man from the Enemy. It does not matter how small the sins are provided that their cumulative effect is to edge the man away from the Light and out into the Nothing. Murder is no better than cards if cards can do the trick. Indeed the safest road to

Hell is the gradual one—the gentle slope, soft underfoot, without sudden turnings, without milestones, without signposts.[4]

All of us have particular snares in our lives, and the bait is probably different for each of us. Each craving is unique, and we can be certain that Satan has scattered bait all around our lives to entice us. We are not called to live in fear but in caution. Sin desires us and just keeps changing the bait in our lives until we find ourselves with no escape.

4 C. S. Lewis, *The Screwtape Letters* (1942; repr., New York: HarperOne, 2001), 60–61.

8

THE AMBITIOUS PRIEST

Text: Judges 17

In the autumn of 1942 after the decisive victory in North Africa against Rommel, Winston Churchill said, "Now this is not the end. It is not even the beginning of the end. But it is, perhaps, the end of the beginning."[5] In the same way, Judges 17–18 points to the end of the beginning—the exodus from Egypt, the giving of the Law, surviving the wilderness, and coming into Canaan. It is a hinge point in the story of Israel because it is the precursor to the eventual annihilation of the Northern tribes and the exile of Judah in Babylon. Here we have all the clues of what will in time cause Israel to fall in on itself hundreds of years later. All great failures begin with the corruption of character.

It's all one account, but spread out in two chapters. Like a good television script, it is two subplots that converge at the end. The characters in the course of the story "connect the dots," and we end with a tale that manages to weave everything together.

Section 1—Judges 17
We begin with two relationships: Micah (not Micah the prophet) and his

---

5   https://winstonchurchill.org/the-life-of-churchill/war-leader/1940-1942/autumn-1942-age-68/

mother; and then Micah and the young unnamed Levite. This forms the spine of the story.

Micah loved money and stole silver from his mother, but he returns it to her. Then she genuinely thinks her dedicating the silver to make an idol is consistent with her religious beliefs.

How does that happen? How do people get so confused when the commandment is so clear? First, it was a time when every man did what was right in their own eyes. Second, the mother did not follow sound teaching; rather she practiced beliefs that slowly moved people to distorted theology. We see the same today when people are disconnected from sound teaching and accountability. It's never sudden. It's gradual . . . and always makes sense but ends in confusion.

Micah is as confused and deluded as his mother. He invites a young Levite from Bethlehem to live with him as a son and be his priest. Micah ordains his "son," and then we see what happens when faith becomes superstition. A relationship becomes a transaction and a formula for success. That is why Micah says, "I know that the LORD will be good to me, since this Levite has become my priest" (17:13).

The unnamed Levite is a young and ambitious religious entrepreneur. He is restless in a small town and wants something more—a position and a relationship with a wealthy man and his family. He has mistaken a calling for a career.

According to the NIV, Micah "installed" the young priest (v. 12)—other translations use "ordained" or "consecrated." It was not something to be taken lightly. Eugene Peterson writes about the vow that those in ministry must make to their people when they are ordained. It is not just ministers. It is all of us in any kind of ministry—like teaching Sunday school. That's why I keep this copy signed by Eugene in my Bible.

> One more thing: we are going to ordain you to this ministry and we want your vow that you will stick to it. This is not a temporary job assignment but a way of life that we need lived out in our community. We know

that you are launched on the same difficult belief venture in the same dangerous world as we are. We know that your emotions are as fickle as ours. That is why we are going to ordain you and why we are going to exact a vow from you.[6]

In this first chapter you see all the basic themes in the rest of the story: disloyalty, confusion, isolation, and people deciding themselves what is right and wrong—and then covering it with all kinds of God language.

Section 2: Judges 18:1–26

The Danites are unsuccessful in conquering the Canaanites in the territory assigned to them and are looking for an easy way out. They are looking for easy prey and a hostile takeover, so they find an accommodating Levite who will tell them what they want to hear—they want God's approval, and he gives it to them. They are not looking for guidance but for permission and they have come to the right place. "He has hired me and I am his priest," the Levite says regarding Micah. He encourages them to take advantage of these "unsuspecting people" (v. 10) and to think God has put them into their hands. More God language. When they are leaving, they say to the Levite: "'Come with us, and be our father and priest. Isn't it better that you serve a tribe and clan in Israel as priest rather than just one man's household?' Then the priest was very pleased. He took the ephod, the household gods and the idol and went along with the people" (18:19–20).

Section 3: Judges 18:27–31

Now the "big reveal" happens in the identity of the Levite priest, and it is the saddest irony in the story. He is Jonathan, the son of Gershom, the son of Moses. *His grandfather is Moses.*

When Moses gave commands to the Levites years earlier, he could not have imagined it would be his own family that would destroy what he had accomplished:

---

6 Eugene H. Peterson, *Working the Angles: The Shape of Pastoral Integrity* (Grand Rapids: Wm. B. Eerdmans Publishing Co., 1987), 24.

"Take this Book of the Law and place it beside the ark of the covenant of the LORD your God. There it will remain as a witness against you. . . . For I know that after my death you are sure to become utterly corrupt and to turn from the way I have commanded you. In days to come, disaster will fall on you because you will do evil in the sight of the LORD and arouse his anger by what your hands have made." (Deut. 31:24–29)

The end result of Jonathan's lack of character is the destruction and enslavement of Israel. As we know, the ten tribes go into captivity and completely disappear from history. The ultimate effect of the grandson's life is the unraveling of his grandfather's lifework. Though unintentional, it was still a tragedy. The combination of so many small elements leads to the end of a nation—self-indulgence, isolation, disloyalty, pride, misuse of power, distorted theology, and ambition over time brings down an entire country. It was not obvious. It's beginning seemed like such an insignificant thing—a mother's confusion and a spoiled son. But, as in our own lives, one thing leads to another that we could never predict.

Each one of us, in some part, is described in this account. We all struggle with these temptations:

- Like the mother, we are tempted to exchange the truth of God for a lie.
- Like Micah, we try to manipulate God into blessing us.
- Like Jonathan, we want a larger opportunity and more influence and better associations.
- Think about what safeguards you need to work into your life to avoid these things. Far more than you imagine may be depending on your personal integrity.

9

STOLEN HEARTS

Text: 2 Samuel 15

Rebellions do not happen overnight. After years, there is always a tipping point in either an event or a moment that precipitates them. We talk about the beginnings of the American Revolution and we know it was not simply the Boston Tea Party or the Boston Massacre, but the years of resentment over the taxes Britain imposed to maintain their troops after the French-Indian War and to increase revenue for a Parliament strapped for cash by an exploding national debt. There was a twelve-year buildup to the American Revolution.

It is true for Absalom's rebellion as well. Look at the numbers:

- After the rape of his sister Tamar, he spent two years waiting and planning for his revenge on Amnon.

- He spent three years in exile in his grandfather's house in Geshur after executing Amnon.

- Brought back to Jerusalem through the intrigue and deception of Joab, he spent two years in isolation. In that time, he had a child he named Tamar. (That should have been a clue.)

- He spent four years sitting at the gate of the city positioning himself as an advocate for the people.

That's a total of eleven years that Absalom prepared for what became a revolt against his father, David.

At some point along the way Absalom reached a tipping point in his desire to punish his father for his abdicating his duty to deal with Amnon for raping Tamar.

But David began abdicating his responsibilities long before that. Our first indication is in 2 Samuel 11 by his remaining in Jerusalem while his men were in battle against the Ammonites. Armies need leadership, and David was either bored or distracted.

Something happens to David's heart and spirit after the adultery with Bathsheba. There is a sense of fatalism and resignation we never saw in the young David. There is something going on in David's soul. He has lost his taste for leading, resigning himself to the consequences of his sin. Even in his response to the rape of Tamar, there are no teeth in his anger (2 Sam. 13:21).

While David may not have seen it coming because either it was hidden from him by those around him or he refused to acknowledge it, the worst events of his life are on the horizon. He is about to be overthrown and forced to flee for his life.

> In the course of time, Absalom provided himself with a chariot and horses and with fifty men to run ahead of him. He would get up early and stand by the side of the road leading to the city gate. Whenever anyone came with a complaint to be placed before the king for a decision, Absalom would call out to him, "What town are you from?" He would answer, "Your servant is from one of the tribes of Israel." Then Absalom would say to him, "Look, your claims are valid and proper, but there is no representative of the king to hear you." And Ab-

salom would add, "If only I were appointed judge in the land! Then everyone who has a complaint or case could come to me and I would see that they receive justice." Also, whenever anyone approached him to bow down before him, Absalom would reach out his hand, take hold of him and kiss him. Absalom behaved in this way toward all the Israelites who came to the king asking for justice, and so he stole the hearts of the people of Israel. (2 Sam. 15:1–6)

How do you steal the hearts of an entire people?

1. **You begin with a particular set of circumstances.** Clearly, the courts are clogged and people are bringing their cases to be tried and getting no response from David or his judges.

2. **You let that pot simmer for a few years until there is a general atmosphere of resentment** and, like the beginnings of the American Revolution, the dissatisfaction of not being heard or respected. People no longer believe in the system. They don't believe it is fair. They don't believe their leaders are interested in their lives.

3. **There is typically an individual who steps into this bubbling resentment and takes advantage of the mistrust and grievance.** Normally, it is someone with a well-developed sense of grievance themselves. It is someone like Absalom who has been nursing this cold anger for years and waiting for the right moment. They do not simply describe or understand what people feel; they give people a vocabulary for their grudges and resentments, which only fires them up further. They justify the rage and direct it toward an enemy. Sometimes the enemy has a face, but it is often just "those people."

4. **This self-announced leader creates a presence and aura that makes people notice them and give them credibility.** They are not openly rebellious, but they are ostentatious about their growing influence. Absalom's chariot and fifty men were a bold way of declaring himself a prince and causing people to notice him. It gave him a platform and

an image that was indelible. Absalom was determined to be recognized for who he thought himself to be.

5. **The new leader has the answer, a solution.** "If only I were appointed judge in the land! Then everyone who has a complaint or case could come to me and I would see that he gets justice." Almost always, justice means at the expense of someone who is increasingly perceived as the enemy. First, you have to encourage their sense of being deprived of justice, and then you have to identify those who are keeping it from them. Lastly, you propose a simple solution that, of course, gives ultimate power to the new leader. In *How Democracies Die* we read, "Populists tend to deny the legitimacy of established parties, attacking them as undemocratic and even unpatriotic. They tell voters that the existing system is not really a democracy but instead has been hijacked, corrupted, or rigged by the elite. And they promise to bury that elite and return power to 'the people.'"[7]

6. **They insinuate themselves into the trust of the people** and make them think, *He speaks for me. He understands me. He is not treating me like the elites do. He is one of us.* Absalom did not seize the reins of power. He stood between the people and the rightful but declining king and listened to them while convincing them he was the only one who could treat them fairly and make certain they received justice. In spite of the wealth, chariots, uncontrollable anger, narcissism, scores of pleasers around him, and vanity, he believed he was their savior.

How do kings lose power? How do autocrats steal the hearts of people and take over? How do democracies die? People lose their faith in them. They abdicate their responsibilities. They become unresponsive and tired. So, people look for someone to take care of them and to follow. They look for certainty and someone who will be one of them to protect their interests. And, in the end, they become sheep. Absalom won their hearts, but the wheel of justice moves slowly but grinds exceedingly fine.

---

7   Steven Levitsky and Daniel Ziblatt, *How Democracies Die* (New York: Crown Publishing, 2018), 22.

10

MAN OF THE PEOPLE

Text: 1 Kings 11–12

Have you ever noticed the number of stories Jesus tells about a king, a ruler, or a master who goes away and leaves people with instructions about how to live in his absence? The result is the same: an individual believes he knows better than the master. *Do I really have to follow the instructions to a T? Surely there is some wiggle room.* It is a corruption of character. That is what the Bible means when it says there was a "sin of the house" of a person (1 Kings 13:34). It was not just that person alone but that sin became a character trait of generations of his descendants. It became the sin that defined them and, in time, was the seed of their destruction.

Jeroboam was yet another man who thought he could "sort of" follow God's commands. It is not just the sins of Jeroboam but the sin of the house of Jeroboam that led to the destruction of Israel.

Years later, the divided kingdom of Israel and Judah lasts 241 years after Solomon. During that time there are sixteen kings of the Northern Kingdom from Jeroboam to the last king, Hoshea. The final commentary on many of those kings is "he did what was evil in the sight of the LORD and walked in the way of Jeroboam" (1 Kings 15:34 ESV). Even if they did good things, "he walked in the ways of Jeroboam" is the final obituary on every leader for hundreds of years.

What is this defining sin, the standard by which all kings come to be judged?

What is the sin of the house of Jeroboam, and does it have any relevance for us today?

We find the story of this promising young leader in 1 Kings 11:28. "Now Jeroboam was a man of standing, and when Solomon saw how well the young man did his work, he put him in charge of the whole labor force of the tribes of Joseph." Jeroboam knew how to manage and get things done. He knew how to motivate and lead people and how to inspire the confidence of others—especially the rulers. In fact, his very name means "man of the people"—a populist and not an aristocrat.

Then, as is often the case with people God chooses, comes a turning point through an encounter with a prophet. God picks Jeroboam out and promises him that he will be the ruler of ten tribes. "I will take the kingdom from his son's hands and give you ten tribes. . . . I will take you, and you will rule over all that your heart desires; you will be king over Israel. If you do whatever I command you and walk in obedience to me and do what is right in my eyes by obeying my decrees and commands . . . I will be with you. I will build you a dynasty as enduring as the one I built for David and will give Israel to you" (1 Kings 11:35, 37–38).

Naturally and predictably, King Solomon tries to kill him and Jeroboam flees to Egypt and stays there until Solomon's death. So far, it's a classic story of biblical calling—Moses, David, Jesus, Paul. A promise, opposition, leaving, and returning.

When Solomon dies, Jeroboam returns and there is the inevitable confrontation with Solomon's son and rightful heir—Rehoboam. Rehoboam is harsh and prideful while being assured of his own invincibility by foolish advisors. Led by Jeroboam, the people revolt and break off into a separate kingdom.

So far, there is no sin. In fact, just the opposite. Jeroboam is doing just as God instructed.

Then comes the next turning point—which proves fatal not only to him but to all of his successors. Jeroboam, like the rich fool, consults himself only and then leans on his own understanding of practical politics and the counsel from his political advisors. He puts being a man of the people over being a man of God and his desire to retain power over his responsibility to retain principle. He convinces himself that God cannot do what he said he would do. Remember what made Abraham a man of faith? He was fully persuaded that God had power to do what he had promised" (Rom. 4:21).

Jeroboam devises a brilliant strategy to protect his interests and perceptive reading of the nature of people. He does not outlaw religion. He does not use force to control the people. He recognizes the power of easy religion to shape people. He makes them consumers of convenience and choice. He uses religion with only a few changes that are reasonable for everyone.

Why make the long, expensive and dangerous journey to Jerusalem when you can worship closer to where you live with people you trust?

Why support an institution that tells you what to do when you can have a religion that is more compatible with what you want—and deserve?

And here is the brilliance of it. They believed it. He was able to sell them on the possibility of holding two opposite standards in their minds with no thought of the consequences. They trusted him. After all, he was a man of the people.

We can disobey God and at the same time live blessed lives.

We can serve idols with none of the unpleasant aftertaste.

People tend to resolve two things in conflict in a way that eliminates the discomfort without having to choose one or the other. So, they find a way to choose both—they combine them.

Everything was fine at first. But the Scripture says, "And this thing became a sin . . ." (1 Kings 12:30). Over time their choices became not only a sin but a sin so corrosive that it led eventually to the destruction of Jeroboam's whole family and the nation itself.

What was at first merely an accommodation to people became a horror. "They bowed down to all the starry hosts, and they worshiped Baal. They sacrificed their sons and daughters in the fire. They practiced divination and sought omens and sold themselves to do evil in the eyes of the LORD, arousing him to anger" (2 Kings 17:16–17).

Even the best kings could not change what Jeroboam did. It was a permanent characteristic and practice of the people. It had become so woven into their character that no change in leadership could pull it out without unraveling the whole. I'm reminded of the parable of the wheat and the tares (Matt. 13:24–30). There was no way to separate what the Enemy had sown without uprooting the good, so they both had to grow together until the time came to harvest. Unfortunately, the harvest was the end of the nation. And it all was traced back to the sin of the house of Jeroboam.

The concessions we make today regarding following God's ways can have repercussions in our families—our houses—for generations to come. "Trust in the LORD with all your heart and lean not on your own understanding; in all your ways submit to him, and he will make your paths straight" (Prov. 3:5–6).

II

PLANT A TREE

Text: Psalm 1

I love trees—especially oak trees. I suppose that is why I chose an oak tree for the logo for both The Gathering and the Fourth Partner Foundation years ago. Everything I wanted to say about them was summed up in a tree— and especially a tree by a stream as we find it here:

> Blessed is the one
> who does not walk in step with the wicked
> or stand in the way that sinners take
> or sit in the company of mockers,
> but whose delight is in the law of the LORD,
> and who meditates on his law day and night.
> That person is like a tree planted by streams of water,
> which yields its fruit in season
> and whose leaf does not wither—
> whatever they do prospers.
> Not so the wicked!
> They are like chaff
> that the wind blows away.
> Therefore the wicked will not stand in the judgment,
> nor sinners in the assembly of the righteous.
> For the LORD watches over the way of the righteous,
> but the way of the wicked leads to destruction. (Ps. 1)

For me, a tree has been a symbol for several important traits:

1. **It is a symbol of productivity**. A tree turns water into fruit for others. A tree provides shade for the weary. A tree is a haven for birds. A tree improves the life of everything to which it is connected. The common English Oak can support hundreds of different species, including 284 species of insect and 324 species of lichens living directly on the tree. These in turn provide food for numerous birds and small mammals. The acorns of oak trees are food for dozens of species, including wild boar, jays, pigeons, pheasants, ducks, squirrels, mice, badgers, and deer. A tree is the center of a whole community of living things.

Even when it is cut down it provides wood for fire and timber for houses. I had a friend who once said he wanted to be as productive as a tree. "I'll produce fruit for as long as I can . . . and then you can make a writing desk out of me."

When the Bible talks about prosperity, it means to produce something—not just to accumulate wealth. It is more like completing the task you have been assigned in a way that is useful to God and others. That, of course, is what healthy (prosperous) trees and people do. They fulfill their purpose. They do their job.

2. **It is a reminder of gratitude**. Someone likely planted that tree by the water. As well, they both, in a way, give each other life. The tree draws life from the stream but in doing so it gives the stream something of a purpose and allows it to leave something tangible behind instead of just passing through on its way to the sea.

3. **It is a symbol of the delight that good work produces**. Not just work for money or work that is mere drudgery but work that suits us. The kind of work that creates justifiable pride and satisfaction. It's trite perhaps but I have liked the phrase, "Find what you love to do and you will never work a day in your life." It does not mean what you love to do will be easy or effortless. Good work is hard. It is difficult and demanding but it is satisfying. Still, I think the apostle Paul was right when he told the church at Thessalonica that the way to live was to "make it your ambition to lead a quiet life, to

mind your own business and to work with your hands . . . so that your daily life may win the respect of outsiders . . ." (1 Thess. 4:11–12).

4. It is a reminder of the seasons—good and difficult—in life. When we study the rings inside a tree, we can see the evidence of fire, flood, and infestation—all the things that attack the life. We can also mark the times of growth and health. I would love to see the rings of some of you! What were the good times and the times that nearly took you down? When did you grow and when did you struggle?

5. A tree is an example of rootedness. It is committed to where it lives and does not move around. A whole ecology of relationships grows up around it. And it is not just a commitment to place but a commitment to the people in our lives as well.

I was in a dark theater watching a performance of *Over the River and Through the Woods*. Joe DiPietro scripts the poignant story of an immigrant Italian family in New York whose grandson Nick has made a decision to move away—far away—to Seattle for his work. The central conflict is the struggle between desiring a personal identity and life separate from family and the reality that our lives are entangled with theirs.

In my conversations with young people, this is the first issue that comes up. *How do I renegotiate my relationship with my parents? How can I encourage them to turn loose of me and me of them?* For the grandparents in the play, their commitment to family is the source of their identity. There is no such thing as an identity outside of family. Time and again they use the phrase *tengo familia* ("I have a family") to describe what it means to have and to be held by family. It's the primary relationship in life, and to take care of and be cared for by family is the basis of a life that is satisfying.

Many of us struggle between taking advantage of opportunities and still being anchored in relationships that constrain us. How much do we owe the people who love us? How much of us belongs to them? How much of ourselves are we willing to give up to belong to family?

Sitting there I remembered a quote from Wendell Berry's book *Jayber*

Crow: "And so I came to belong to this place.... Being here satisfies me. I had laid my claim on the place, had made it answerable to my life. Of course, you can't do that and get away free. You can't choose, it seems, without being chosen. For the place, in return, had laid its claim on me and had made my life answerable to it."[8]

I didn't understand the value of belonging when I was younger. I was always ready to move on. My bag was always packed and the adventure of the next experience was irresistible. Maybe it had something to do with sharing my father's name but making a name for myself kept me pushing out. I did not appreciate as I do now what it means to belong to a place or to have a place and people who lay their claim on me. While I don't think I could have done it differently, I am grateful I have been given this opportunity—the opportunity to belong and to be satisfied in being here.

Like a tree planted by streams of water . . .

---

8 Wendell Berry, *Jayber Crow: The Novel* (Berkeley, CA: Counterpoint, 2001), 36.

12

HIDDEN IN PLAIN SIGHT

| Text: Psalm 78 |

When the psalmist Asaph wrote Psalm 78, he must have been anticipating Stephen Covey and his famous line: "Begin with the end in mind,"[9] because that is exactly what he is doing. In other words, the psalm is actually best read from the bottom to the top or from the last lines to the first.

It is a long psalm and written to make points about the history and character of Israel, their God and Israel's king. Everything else, from the beginning to the end, is making the case for the conclusion in the last two verses:

> He chose David his servant and took him from the sheep pens; from tending the sheep he brought him to be the shepherd of his people Jacob, of Israel his inheritance. And David shepherded them with integrity of heart; with skillful hands he led them. (vv. 71–72)

So, let's go to the beginning to read the psalm now that we know what the psalmist has in his mind: the goodness of God in making David the leader of Israel.

---

9   Stephen R. Covey, *The 7 Habits of Highly Effective People* (New York: Simon & Schuster, 1989), 109.

> I will open my mouth with a parable; I will utter hidden things, things from of old—things we have heard and known, things our ancestors have told us. We will not hide them from their descendants; we will tell the next generation. (vv. 2–3)

Sometimes things have been heard and known in the past but have been intentionally hidden. Hiding the truth and hiding from the truth has been a pattern of mankind from the very beginning. We try to hide them because they are uncomfortable and make us look bad. We want to make up a history that will make us look better. In Scott Peck's *People of the Lie*, he writes that each family has a lie that they pass on from one generation to the next. They may not even be able to articulate it, but it shapes them because they spend their lives hiding something about themselves or avoiding something that is unpleasant to face. So the psalmist says, "we will not hide them from their descendants; we will tell the next generation . . ." (v. 4). That would not sit well with people who wanted their history to be scrubbed and polished.

What then are we to tell the next generation? Two things:

First, we are to tell them the praiseworthy deeds of the Lord, his power, and the wonders he has done. God is real in our lives.

Second, we are to tell them the laws he has established so they would know and follow them after us.

I think it was true for Israel then and for us now that we have become so infatuated with our own wonders that we have stopped considering the wonders and deeds of the Lord. The mystery is gone. Not only has our sense of wonder been reduced, but we have replaced the laws and statutes with our own principles and our own "isms." We need things more practical and less restrictive.

Ironically, we have not covered up those commands as much as we have hidden them in plain sight. Over 100 million Bibles are printed every year and 87 percent of U.S. homes own one, yet Lifeway Research found that about half of Americans have read little to none of the Bible.[10] The commands and statutes are on the bookshelf but hidden.

And because of our loss of both wonder and knowledge about Scripture, our children and theirs are losing their trust in God. In other words, *there must be both a relationship with God as well as an ability to obey his commands.* It cannot be one to the exclusion of the other. "God loves me and that's enough" leads to a faith that never grows up. "God loves me only when I am obedient" leads to a faith that is dry and unhealthy.

Psalm 78 is not so much instruction about what our children should do as it is about telling the truth about ourselves and our own history. That is why the bulk of the psalm is a scathing indictment about the character of the people of Israel and their continuing history of disobedience and rebellion. Who wants to hear words like *stubborn, rebellious, disloyal, unfaithful, forgetful, turning back, cowardly, demanding, craving, disbelieving, untrusting, flattering, lying, unreliable,* and *idolatrous*?

No surprise that the people have kept these things hidden for so long! But that is exactly what the writer is doing in uncovering the true nature of the people of Israel. Even worse, he has turned it into music which is then sung repeatedly in worship. Instead of "What a Friend We Have in Jesus," they are singing "In spite of all this, they kept on sinning; In spite of his wonders, they did not believe. So he ended their days in futility and their years in terror" (vv. 32–33). I imagine people figured out when THAT was going to be on the program and skipped that service! We want to feel better about ourselves when we leave church—not worse.

But that is precisely the point. This is not about making things great again. Things have never been great, but we've been great at trying to keep them hidden. The psalm is not about greatness or God's desire to make us comfortable and happy. No, it is about the depth of the sinful nature and the

---

10   "Americans Are Fond of the Bible, Don't Actually Read It," April 25, 2017, https://lifewayresearch.com/2017/04/25/lifeway-research-americans-are-fond-of-the-bible-dont-actually-read-it/.

incomprehensible patience and love of God for reprehensible people who turn away from him over and over again and then ask, "What have you done for me lately?"

God does not love them because they have done anything to deserve it. Just the opposite. He bears with them because he has made an everlasting covenant with them. That is why the psalm closes as it does. It is the one bright spot in their whole history, isn't it? Out of his love God did not give them a lion tamer or a cowboy or a snake charmer. He gives them the shepherd David— because they are sheep. Over and over again that is Scripture's description of us—we are wandering and lost sheep.

God gives them what they cannot create and what they would never choose for themselves. He anoints a man who was himself hidden and not anyone's choice—except God's. But God gives undeserving people the very best, and the whole psalm is written to show that.

In some ways, it is a picture of the history of the church as well. We crave things. We flatter and lie. We are filled with wonder at what we have done and we devise our own statutes and commands for people to follow. We hide the only truth that will give the next generation life and keep them from being stubborn and rebellious.

But in spite of that, God gives us "the bread of angels" (v. 25) and forgives our iniquities and infidelity. He has given us a shepherd for our souls, as the apostle Peter puts it (1 Pet. 2:25). He has given us the best as undeserving as we are. He is faithful even we are not.

13

COMMON PRAISE

🐚

Text: Psalm 148

As we get older, we tend to focus on what matters most. I've thought about that when I look at the last six psalms David wrote. All of them begin with "Hallelujah" or "Praise the LORD." They all are reflections on the larger themes of life and the faithfulness of God through it all. "Blessed are those whose help is the God of Jacob. whose hope is in the LORD his God. He is the Maker of heaven and earth, the sea, and everything in them—he remains faithful forever" (Ps. 146:5–6).

I can imagine David re-reading the story of creation in Genesis and being amazed and only able to say to himself "Praise the LORD" because that is how Psalm 148 begins. Is it an essay or a paper or a long treatise on creation? No, David's deepest thoughts and emotions were always expressed by poetry. That's what poetry is for and what it does.

Poet Christopher Fry said, "Poetry is a language in which man explores his own amazement."

That is a good description of Psalm 148. It is David's amazement at God's act of creation put into words.

So David begins with praise and then with the first day of creation. All the created beings who were with God when he created the world are there to praise him—the angels and the heavenly hosts. Praise is not the same as countless millions of angels and heavenly hosts standing around and giving God compliments. It is literally shouting. "Then I heard what sounded like a great multitude, like the roar of rushing waters and like loud peals of thunder, shouting: 'Hallelujah! For our Lord God almighty reigns. Let us rejoice and be glad and give him glory!'" (Rev. 19:6–7).

That means all of creation in one way or another, and in ways we cannot hear, is shouting God's praise! The sun, moon, and stars are all praising God for their very existence. They are not passive and inert.

How are they doing that? Why are we deaf to it?

St. Augustine said: ". . . the beauty of all things is in a manner their voice, whereby they praise God. The heaven crieth out to God, 'Thou madest me, not I myself.' Earth crieth out, 'Thou createdst me, not I myself.' How do they cry out? When thou regardest them, and findest this out, they cry out by thy voice, they cry out by thy regard."[11]

We enable them to praise God just by our noticing them.

Creation is not random or accidental. It is intentional and God spoke it into existence. Created things are more than so much matter in space. They are set in place. They are ordered and to such a degree that the smallest variation would make life impossible.

It is like Job's response: "Surely I spoke of things I did not understand, things too wonderful for me to know" (Job 42:3).

And that (verse 6) is where Psalm 148 transitions from the creation of the heavens to the earth. David moves from the eternal to the temporal and still everything was created to praise God. Paul says that creation "groans" as it awaits redemption (Rom. 8:22). What was once able to sing is now able only

---

11 St. Augustine Bishop of Hippo, *Expositions on the Book of Psalms 101–50* (New Apostolic Bible Covenant, 2019), 300.

to groan, but there is still beauty and order even in a fallen world. It is what Leonard Cohen called the "cold and broken hallelujah" in a piece he wrote in 1984. While it was never recognized for decades, it is now something of an anthem for many artists.

> "This world is full of conflicts and full of things that cannot be reconciled," Cohen has said, "but there are moments when we can transcend the dualistic system and reconcile and embrace the whole mess, and that's what I mean by 'Hallelujah.' That regardless of what the impossibility of the situation is, there is a moment when you open your mouth and you throw open your arms and you embrace the thing and you just say, 'Hallelujah! Blessed is the name.' . . .

> "The only moment that you can live here comfortably in these absolutely irreconcilable conflicts is in this moment when you embrace it all and you say, 'Look, I don't understand . . . at all—Hallelujah!' That's the only moment that we live here fully as human beings."[12]

That's what Paul meant when he said in all things break bread and give thanks. Life is difficult and messy and painful but we still say Hallelujah. It may not be a shout. It may be a whisper or a groan, but we find a way to say God is faithful and we can trust him because we are his.

All creatures great and small praise him. There is nothing insignificant in our world. There are things we overlook or call common but only because we do not see them for what they are. I like the story of silicon—or what we call sand. It is everywhere. It is the seventh most common element in the universe. We use it for the most unremarkable things—like cement or forging steel. But in the last century this unremarkable substance became the key element of integrated circuits and that has changed the world. The

---

12 Alan Light, *The Holy or the Broken: Leonard Cohen, Jeff Buckley and the Unlikely Ascent of "Hallelujah"* (New York: Atria, 2012), 30–31.

world is like that. Common things praise God in unnoticed ways.

I love verse 12 of Psalm 148 because it describes the power of a normal life to praise God—"Young men and women, old men and children." This one phrase describes the whole life of a family. "One generation will commend your works to another" is a good description of our role in the lives of our children and grandchildren (Ps. 145:4).

And then there is a second and final transition. David's poem connects the eternal and the physical. The seen and the unseen. "He has raised up for his people a horn [meaning, strength], the praise of all his faithful servants, of Israel, the people close to his heart" (Ps. 148:14). This whole poem is about Christ and his becoming the visible image of the invisible God—the first-born over all creation.

> The Son is the image of the invisible God, the firstborn over all creation. For in him all things were created: things in heaven and on earth, visible and invisible, whether thrones or powers or rulers or authorities; all things have been created through him and for him. He is before all things, and in him all things hold together. And he is the head of the body, the church; he is the beginning and the firstborn from among the dead, so that in everything he might have the supremacy. For God was pleased to have all his fullness dwell in him, and through him to reconcile to himself all things, whether things on earth or things in heaven, by making peace through his blood, shed on the cross. (Col. 1:15–20)

Hallelujah is how it begins and how it ends. We live in between those two. We live in both amazement and groaning. But we know that all of creation will one day be restored to what it once was and the dwelling of God will be with us.

"Then I heard what sounded like a great multitude, like the roar of rushing waters and like loud peals of thunder, shouting: 'Hallelujah! For our Lord God almighty reigns. Let us rejoice and be glad and give him glory!'" (Rev. 19:6–7).

14

LITTLE FOXES

Text: Song of Solomon 2

Tradition says this text in Song of Solomon is the romance between Solomon and his second wife, Naamah. His first wife from Egypt was basically a political maneuver when he was a young man, and the only wife mentioned by name is his second who was an Ammonite, a foreigner and dark-skinned.

As well, as he had 700 wives and 300 concubines, I find it hard to believe he would have had the energy or creativity to compose such a letter to each of them. Naamah was his first love and the mother of his son, Rehoboam, who became his successor. This is Solomon before his great success, his wandering from the faith, and his dark reflections in the book of Ecclesiastes. These are the words of a young Solomon who only requested wisdom from the Lord that he might rule the people with an understanding heart. "So God said to him . . . 'I will do what you have asked. I will give you a wise and discerning heart. . . . Moreover, I will give you what you have not asked for—both wealth and honor—so that in your lifetime you will have no equal among kings'" (1 Kings 3:11–14).

Our focus in Solomon's letter is on a single verse in chapter 2:

> Catch for us the foxes, the little foxes that ruin the vineyards, our vineyards that are in bloom. (v. 15)

All relationships have issues that threaten to dig up what has been planted. It might be marriage, as it is here between Solomon and Naamah, but it is also friendships, organizations, even countries that become divided and distrustful. There are always little foxes at work. I like the way Harold Martin puts it in "A Warfare with Little Foxes":

> But even this most exquisite marriage relationship had its share of bumps and bruises. Each partner was still a human being with a sin-prone heart. Each one did things to hurt their mate, and each one felt hurt in some way. Chapters 3 and 5 include examples of this. It was the little issues or "foxes" that were spoiling their otherwise happy relationship. Small issues became a big hindrance in this couple's pursuit of total oneness. . . . The little foxes are an example of the kinds of problems which can disturb or destroy a good relationship. . . . What chews away at our lives?[13]

What are the threats in mature marriages and relationships, yet are still in danger of being damaged by "little foxes"?

- **Infidelity** is never out of the question—no matter how old we are. And, it is not always sexual, is it? We can be unfaithful in other ways when we make work or other interests into lovers that draw us away from our spouses and families. For too many ministers the church becomes a mistress and the family is left behind. For others, it may be our career or relationships outside our marriage that are not physical but become emotional affairs. Unfaithfulness, like a pandemic, has no regard for age.

- **Cynicism and resignation** after so many years of being together makes us begin to say, "They will never change. Why even try to hope?" But when we turn it around and think about how it makes us feel when

---

13   Harold S. Martin, "A Warfare with Little Foxes," Bible Helps Booklet #427, November 2016, https://biblehelpsinc.org/publication/a-warfare-with-little-foxes/.

we think the other person is saying that *about us*, we are discouraged. Sometimes we want to change even though it looks like we are defeated every time and we just revert to the old behavior of being defensive or angry or withdrawn. Losing hope in the other person chews away at us over time.

- **Irritability** is another fox. We lose patience and begin to say, "After all this time they know that irritates me but they just keep doing it." Or, we want them to read our minds or talk to us. We don't get angry, really. We just push them away with a look or a comment.

- **Disrespect** chews at our relationships. We take our spouse for granted and feel no remorse at embarrassing or belittling them in public or even throwing them under the bus to save our own self-image. We peck away at their flaws and habits. We focus on the things about which they are most insecure and use those against them.

- **Unkindness** becomes a habit. Years ago, a young man asked me about the key to a successful marriage. Though no expert, I look at kindness—the basis of a good relationship—as a "gateway virtue" that leads to other virtues. Second Peter 1:5–7 shows the progression: "For this very reason, make every effort to add to your faith goodness; and to goodness, knowledge; and to knowledge, self-control; and to self-control, perseverance; and to perseverance, godliness; and to godliness, mutual affection; and to mutual affection, love." It is not a prescription of duties and chores, but a description of a life that grows. There is a beginning—faith—and an end—love. But after faith, *what is the first step toward love?* The Greek word used here, *arete*, is often translated as "kindness or goodness." Kindness is where we begin, and that became, for me, the first rung on the ladder toward maturity.

- The fox of **self-centeredness** is never sleeping. We would rather talk and think about ourselves than the other person, except on special occasions like Mother's Day and Father's Day, birthdays and anniversaries. But other than that, we have ourselves on our minds. The *Gospel Herald* many years ago printed a list, "How to Be Perfectly

Miserable." Among the list of twenty statements were the following:

- *Think about yourself.*
- *Talk about yourself.*
- *Expect to be appreciated.*
- *Be sensitive to slights.*
- *Never forgive a criticism.*
- *Never forget a service you may have rendered.*[14]

- Finally, there is **bitterness**—a root that will surely ruin any relationship.

Few marriages are ruined by the catastrophes of fire, flood, or drought. For most, it is the nibbling away at the soft roots. The work of keeping the little foxes out of the vineyard is never finished. They find gaps in the hedge or gates we've left open. But over time we build habits of the heart that protect what has been planted and keep them from chewing away at our lives.

---

14 https://www.happypublishing.com/blog/how-to-be-perfectly-miserable/

15

GOD'S GOAT

Text: Isaiah 53

I don't know that I have ever seen an image of Jesus that portrays him in such an unattractive as Isaiah 53—one with no beauty and nothing in him that would attract him to us. Not only are we most familiar with inaccurate pictures of Jesus as a light-skinned or lightly tanned Caucasian, but even when he is pictured as a Jew it is always a very handsome and attractive man. I asked a number of people this week to send me images of Jesus as an ugly man with no beauty whatsoever and have not received any responses. What if Isaiah is right and our artists are not? What if Jesus in the flesh was actually a man so ugly and his features so distorted that people turned away from him when they first saw him? If so, then there had to be something about him that overcame that revulsion.

I met a young woman in my first year of teaching who had been born with the most horrid facial deformities I had ever seen. When I first saw her I literally looked away and thought about avoiding her. She was a senior in high school and had undergone seventy-two surgeries on her face. Yet, after only a few weeks I had not only come to a point of accepting her deformities but had discovered why she was perhaps the most popular student in the school. It was not beauty or polish. It was something far deeper than that. It was the beauty of her soul that drew people to her.

I was at a conference in Nashville recently, and every person on the stage was attractive. There is not anything wrong with that, but I know how much we in the audience value that and how much pressure there is on speakers, pastors, worship leaders to be people whose physical presence does not make us look down in our laps when they are up front. It would be difficult for us not to be distracted by someone whose "appearance was so disfigured beyond that of any man and his form marred beyond human likeness" (Isa. 53:14).

I know how many interpret these verses as his appearance after the beatings and the effects of the crucifixion, but I have begun to think all of the images of Jesus we have are just wrong. I think Isaiah is describing Jesus as he came to us in the flesh. And I think his beauty was the same as that of my student. He grew up like a root out of dry ground—not like a tree planted by a stream.

Paul writes about our being jars of clay (2 Cor. 4:7). I grew up believing the phrase described our frailty or our disposition toward our weakness. However, I think it comes closer to saying we are containers of treasure who appear to be unremarkable but have been given a responsibility to carry the greatest power ever conceived. God has chosen the ordinary—even the ugly—to convey the miraculous.

I've been thinking about the power of the ordinary and the freedom it gives us when we do not have to be the "treasure." Too often, the church has preferred ornate Fabergé eggs to clay pots. We want our leaders to be polished, articulate, and successful in ministry. We encourage them to be anything but ordinary or unremarkable.

Yet, being ordinary allows us to trust in the power of the plain gospel to accomplish its work. We don't need exquisite techniques, production quality experiences, and sophisticated strategies to witness the effects of the gospel. What we do need is to deflect the attention from ourselves and avoid the temptation to become a part of the treasure itself.

It is exactly the power of the ordinary to conceal the extraordinary that is at the heart of J. R. R. Tolkien's *Lord of the Rings*. The Ring was "quite plain" and it was that very feature fooling everyone and allowing it to remain hidden—especially from those who desired to possess it. And, like the Ring, those who want to possess the treasure or use the treasure or even resist being ordinary, are lost. They are destroyed by envy, greed, power, and pride.

But the good news is the power of the treasure we carry, while a constant surprise to others and ourselves will, over time, change us from the inside out. We remain ordinary but are becoming more and more like the gift itself. We are being transformed into his likeness with ever-increasing glory.

Isaiah 53:7 says, "He was oppressed and afflicted, yet he did not open his mouth; he was led like a lamb to the slaughter, and as a sheep before its shearers is silent, so he did not open his mouth." While Jesus is often referred to as the lamb of God who takes away the sins of the world, this whole passage is a reference not just to lambs but to goats. It is a reference to the Day of Atonement. Jesus is the goat of God and that is a much different image, isn't it?

In Leviticus 16 we read about the two goats presented to the Lord: one for a sacrifice and one for a scapegoat for sin. "[Aaron] is to lay both hands on the head of the live goat and confess over it all the wickedness and rebellion of the Israelites—all their sins—and put them on the goat's head. He shall send the goat away into the wilderness in the care of someone appointed for the task. The goat will carry on itself all their sins to a remote place; and the man shall release it in the wilderness" (vv. 21–22).

Christ is both the sacrifice and the goat that carries away our sin. Sin is real and it has to be laid on something and carried far away where we cannot get to it. Corrie Ten Boom said "God has put our sins into the deepest ocean and posted a sign saying, 'No fishing allowed.'"[15]

That is the picture we see in Gethsemane. Christ is being loaded up with the sin of the world. It is not just the anticipated agony of the cross but the separation from the Father and bearing the sin of the world into the wilderness that is his burden that night.

---

15   Corrie Ten Boom, *Tramp for the Lord* (Grand Rapids: Fleming H. Revell Co., 1974), 53.

In warfare there is a term we call "concentration of forces." It is a strategy in which an attacking army puts all of its efforts on a single point in the defenses of the enemy. Once accomplished, the army can use the breach to overwhelm the enemy. That is exactly what I believe Satan did that night in Gethsemane. All the sin of the world was laid on Jesus, and Satan hoped to attack his flank and overwhelm him with despair. But the goat carries our sin into the wilderness.

You are forgiven because Christ bore our sins. And, like him, we will rise to a new life, and the beautiful treasure that we carry within us—our jars of clay—will be revealed.

16

FORGETTING AND REMEMBERING

Text: Isaiah 54

Some of us are getting to the age where we have trouble remembering and an easy time forgetting. While there are far more times in Scripture where God commands us to remember, there are at least two places where we are encouraged to forget certain things.

The first is in Isaiah 54:4: "Do not be afraid; you will not be put to shame. Do not fear disgrace; you will not be humiliated. You will forget the shame of your youth and remember no more the reproach of your widowhood." God is intent that we forget things for which we are ashamed and not to dredge them up or go back and rework them in our minds.

The second is Philippians 3:12–13: "Not that I have already obtained all this, or have already arrived at my goal, but I press on to take hold of that for which Christ Jesus took hold of me. Brothers and sisters, I do not consider myself yet to have taken hold of it. But one thing I do: Forgetting what is behind and straining toward what is ahead."

God wants us to forget what is behind . . . and Paul had quite a bit behind him, didn't he? I remember standing at the back of a cruise ship a couple of years ago thinking that was no way to enjoy the cruise—watching the wake and the gulls feeding on the garbage. I know people who live that way. They live at the back of the boat and only focus on what has happened in their lives—for good or ill. They live watching the wake of where they have been.

Before we look at what God wants us to remember, what are some things remembering is NOT?

- Remembering is not just memorizing. Memorizing is important, but it is not the same. It is memorizing the notes but not the joy of music.

- Remembering is not reminiscing about the past. God does not want us to live in the past—no matter how good we think it was.

- Remembering is not melancholy or dwelling on regrets.

- Remembering in Scripture is not an anchor that keeps us from moving ahead but a keel that keeps us balanced and steady.

What are the things God wants us to remember and not forget?

First, *he wants us to remember him.* Everything else is built on that. "You may say to yourself, 'My power and the strength of my hands have produced this wealth for me.' But remember the LORD your God, for it is he who gives you the ability to produce wealth, and so confirms his covenant, which he swore to your ancestors, as it is today'" (Deut. 8:17–18).

Second, *remember a particular time.* "Only be careful, and watch yourselves closely so that you do not forget the things your eyes have seen or let them fade from your heart as long as you live. Teach them to your children and to their children after them" (Deut. 4:9). I suspect many of us have memories of particular times when God spoke or we were "close to the mountain" and aware of his presence. We should not file those times away and forget them. We cannot live there. We move on. But we remember them and we talk about them with our children and grandchildren.

Third, *remember who you are and where you came from.* I know a few people who would like to forget where they grew up. They are ashamed of it and would like to get as far from their upbringing as possible. Others have strayed from their positive heritage, becoming disconnected—rootless.

Fourth, *remember how the Lord leads.* God's way of leading is not always the easy road. "Remember how the LORD God led you all the way in the wilderness these forty years to humble and test you in order to know what was in your heart, whether or not you would keep his commands" (Deut. 8:2–5).

Fifth, *remember your rebellion.* The Israelites, like us, were easily distracted and prone to wander, and our natural inclination is to be drawn away by other things. Remembering this helps us when that pull happens again.

How do we do this?

It is a lot like candle dipping. It is layer upon layer of obedience in the little things that eventually build up to a life of wisdom. Making candles is such a good illustration for a life of wisdom. By dipping and cooling repeatedly, over time the candle grows until it is ready to fulfill its real purpose—light— and then melt away completely consumed.

Scripture instructs us how to remember all that God has done and pass down his words as a legacy to our families:

> Love the LORD your God with all your heart and with all your soul and with all your strength. These commandments that I give you today are to be on your hearts. Impress them on your children. Talk about them when you sit at home and when you walk along the road, when you lie down and when you get up. Tie them as symbols on your hands and bind them on your foreheads. Write them on the doorframes of your houses and on your gates. (Deut. 6:5–9)

Impress them on your children . . . and your grandchildren. The role of grandparents is to "impress" when parents cannot or do not. It is never too late to speak truth into your kids. No matter how old they are or how much you might feel you missed your chance, there is always a "soft spot" in their hearts that is impressionable and ready to hear from you.

Don't spout Bible verses as pat answers to questions or give incessant lecturing, but make God's truth and his presence a part of the fabric of life—woven into each day but not overdone. More like breathing . . . Jesus tells us in the Great Commission that we are to be making disciples as we go—in the normal course of life and not as a special project.

We all use things around the house as memory aids—notes on the door or refrigerator to remind us to pick up the laundry or change the oil. Create an intentional note that simply says, "Remember who you are and where you come from . . ."

17

THE PRESENT PROBLEM

Text: Isaiah 58

As with most good stories or lessons, it helps to have a little context . . . a back story. In Isaiah 55 the Lord invites the people to come to him and be healed:

> "Come, all you who are thirsty, come to the waters" (v. 1).
> "Give ear and come to me; listen, that you may live" (v. 3).
> "Seek the LORD while he may be found; call on him while he is near" (v. 6).

Then in chapter 57 he rebukes those who do wicked things:

> "The righteous perish, and no one takes it to heart" (v. 1).
> "Who are you mocking? At whom do you sneer and stick out your tongue? Are you not a brood of rebels, the offspring of liars?" (v. 4).
> "'There is no peace,' says my God, 'for the wicked.'" (v. 21).

And then we come to our text—Isaiah 58—which we can divide roughly into three parts:

1. The Hypocrisy of the People
2. What God Defines as Worship
3. The Promise of Healing

The Hypocrisy of the People

In Texas we have a phrase: "all hat and no cattle"—another way of saying "it's all talk." Isaiah writes of the hypocrisy: "Day after day they seek me out; they seem eager to know my ways, as if they were a nation that does what is right and has not forsaken the commands of its God" (58:2). But it is not genuine—"they *seem* to . . ." It is all for show and none of it is real because their hearts are not in it. They want the show of sincerity but not the discipline.

> "Is this the kind of fast I have chosen, only a day for people to humble themselves? Is it only for bowing one's head like a reed and for lying in sackcloth and ashes? Is that what you call a fast, a day acceptable to the LORD?" (v. 5).

Their response in verse 3 questions God's inability to notice them: "Why have we fasted and you have not seen it?" In other words, "When do we get what's coming to us?"

What God Defines as Worship

It is easy to quote verses like 2 Chronicles 7:14: "If my people, who are called by my name, will humble themselves and pray and seek my face and turn from their wicked ways, then I will hear from heaven and I will forgive their sin and will heal their land." Many people apply that to our own country and believe that God will heal the land if we do those things.

My question is, if we want to apply the words of God to Israel to our own country, then are we willing to apply the rest of it as well? It is more than prayer and repentance. It is obedience to the other commands.

> "Is not this the kind of fasting I have chosen: to loose the chains of injustice and untie the cords of the yoke, to set the oppressed free and break every yoke? Is it not to share your food with the hungry and to provide the poor wanderer with shelter—when you see the naked, to clothe him, and not to turn away from your own flesh and blood?" (Isa. 58:6–7)

The New Testament reiterates this theme: "If anyone has material possessions and sees a brother or sister in need but has no pity on them, how can the love of God be in that person?" (1 John 3:17). Yes, faith without works is dead (James 2:17), but compassion without action becomes dead as well. Our hearts become hardened to the suffering right in front of us.

I recently met a bright young woman—a global thinker—whose ambitious question was how to work in a very lucrative business and save up enough money to be able to make a difference. She was frustrated by the scope of the problems she wanted to solve. I shared with her the words of Edmund Burke, "No one makes a greater mistake than the one who does nothing because they can only do a little." My experience is those who are faithful in little will be faithful in much. That is not just about money but responsibility, perspective, influence, and wisdom. Start small but start. Don't wait for the big solutions.

In the Old Testament time, Israel was made up of families and tribes. People lived close to each other and were often clustered where the poor and the rich were not separated. Yes, there was also, like today, disparity and injustice, but it was almost impossible to make it invisible or to avoid it. It was always present. So, I don't believe Isaiah is talking about global hunger, oppression, and injustice. He is addressing those who are part of a *community*. They could not get away from those problems like we can today. There were no institutions or non-profit organizations or safety nets to catch people when they fell into poverty. Relatives and extended family were responsible for them.

Today we have wonderful organizations that do the work for us and we just send them money or volunteer to supplement the work of the professionals. That's good. It's efficient. But it separates us from the oppressed unless we make great efforts to not grow further and further away from them. We often see poverty as a problem to be solved, a war to be waged, and we have made it into a series of great projects and systems that will fix it. Of course, when we cannot fix something, we tend to blame the failure on those who will not be fixed or we move on to other wars to fight.

I believe Isaiah and all of Scripture is written from the perspective of actually knowing each other and bearing each other's burdens. There will never be a substitute for true compassion in action. After all, Jesus said, "Then the King will say to those on his right, '. . . For I was hungry and you gave me something to eat, I was thirsty and you gave me something to drink, I was a stranger and you invited me in, I needed clothes and you clothed me, I was sick and you looked after me, I was in prison and you came to visit me.'"

The best part of that is they did not even realize they had done it. They simply lived their lives in such a way that when the opportunity presented itself, they acted on their faith without show or premeditation—their response came naturally.

The Healing of the Land
Rather than noisy activity or empty practices, true healing results from becoming so aligned with the Spirit of God that the faithful become known as the people who repair what has been broken and restore the places where people dwell. Was there ever a time of such great opportunity as now to be those kinds of people?

May it be said of us that we did not make a show of our obedience or fight for power but, with no recognition at all, our compassion became action.

18

SOFT ON SIN

Text: *The Book of Jonah*

What the heck was Jonah's problem with Nineveh?

The same problem as the older brother in the parable of the prodigal son. The same problem as Job and Jeremiah and David. In fact, the same problem all of us have. How can God be inconsistent? How can he be soft toward the rebellious and so strict with those of us who try so hard to do what is right?

We need Psalm 37 to be true. We need to know that in the end the wicked will get their due and we will get ours. We need to know God does not have a double standard and that he is not fooled by those who are evil. We need to know they do not have him wrapped around their fingers like they do everyone else. If these things are not true, then something is wrong. We cannot be sure of God's own commitment to goodness and fairness.

> Do not fret because of those who are evil or be envious of those who do wrong; for like the grass they will soon wither, like green plants they will soon die away. Trust in the LORD and do good; dwell in the land and enjoy safe pasture. Delight yourself in the LORD and he will give you the desires of your heart. Commit your way to the LORD; trust in him and he will do this: He will make your righteousness shine like the dawn, your

> vindication like the noonday sun. Be still before the LORD and wait patiently for him; do not fret when people succeed in their ways, when they carry out their wicked schemes. . . . A little while, and the wicked will be no more; though you look for them, they will not be found. But the meek will inherit the land and enjoy peace and prosperity. (Ps. 37:1–7, 10–11)

Why be good if God is merciful? Why be righteous if the wicked do not pay in the end? God can be too forgiving. He can offend our sense of justice and common sense. How can we trust him to do what is right? This makes us angry.

Jonah cannot let go of his anger either. It has become a part of his life. It is justified. It is necessary . . . and it is killing him slowly. In fact, he would rather be dead than let go of it. "Now, LORD, take away my life, for it is better for me to die than to live" (Jonah 4:3). I've seen that same anger in people who hate one political party over the other. We like to have someone to resent so we can keep doing things that justify our bitterness.

Jonah needed Nineveh to be wicked because a root of bitterness that needed feeding had grown up in him. The last thing he wanted to do was what God asked him to do—go to Nineveh and speak out against the wrong, confront it—and take the chance that God would forgive. That would offend everything Jonah held to be true. Righteousness is rewarded and unrighteousness is punished.

I would say that you and I have our own Ninevehs—something or someone who deserves our anger and God's, and we have built a small but growing dark area of our lives around our bitterness about them. The Lord said to Jonah, "Is it right for you to be angry?" (v. 4). In a sense God was using Nineveh to change Jonah as much as he was using Jonah to change Nineveh. There are people I consider hypocrites, but they are successful. There are people about whom I enjoy hearing bad news. I absorb the details. I know their flaws and failures and I don't want to see them humbled. I want to see them exposed and found out. If they were truly humbled, they might repent and be even more successful!

And what did Jonah do? He went down when God said go up—down to Joppa, down in the ship, down in the sea, down in the belly of the fish. We cannot stay in the same place when we disobey. Disobedience moves us in the opposite direction from God. We cannot be neutral.

All of us head toward Tarshish or Spain in one way or another when we are running from the terrible freedom of God, the unfairness of God.

To what Spain might you be headed—away from God's call to speak up and bring the possibility of forgiveness? We all prefer running to a place with good people, no inconsistencies, no confrontations, and no hypocrisy. We look for places to start over where no one knows us. No one knows the call we are avoiding. We are looking for a place where good people are blessed and hypocrites are exposed. We want to find a place we can be anonymous and without responsibility—untroubled by obligation or commitments. We will be free to hate what is wrong and love what is good.

I've got bad news for you—we don't get there. Just as it was with Jonah, the whole world seems to conspire against you when you are running from your calling. You are out of your place and that disrupts more than your life alone. It causes everyone around you to be affected.

Where we do get is as far as the belly of a great fish. We don't die. God does not kill us for disobedience nor does he turn his back on us. He puts us in a safe place—a place that saves us from ourselves but not a place he intends for us to stay—a place *between* places. It's not drowning but it's not Nineveh. Some of us are in the belly right now, and maybe we've been there three days, three months, or three years. We are safe—but not satisfied. The belly of the whale is where we wait until we are ready to obey. That could be our work, our family, our ministry, our church.

From what Nineveh might you be running? What justified and legitimate resentment have you been building about someone or something deserving punishment? What kind of Spain is in your mind? A long vacation from people who are hypocrites? Maybe joining a group of people with the same anger and justifying what you feel about those who deserve to be exposed and defeated?

In what great belly might God have you right now? It's a place to wait until you are ready to obey what he has called you to do. We should let go of our anger and run *toward* God's great love rather than away.

19

THE CURE FOR CORRUPTION

Text: Micah 7

Normally, we think of a prophet as calling people to repentance to avoid the judgment of God. But that is not Micah's message. The people are beyond repenting. Instead, they have become fully corrupt—but corrupt in a particular way.

Micah is calling them out for religion with no reality. The people were asking him what more the Lord could require. Did he want them to give more, to sacrifice more, to accept thousands of rams and ten thousand rivers of oil? What more could they do than they were already doing to please the Lord?

God did not want more of their religion. He wanted them to act justly, to love mercy, and to walk humbly with their God (Micah 6:8). They wanted none of that because they had created a religion that allowed them to do the opposite. Their religion covered them when they plotted evil, defrauded a man of his house, and put a woman out of her home for no cause. It was religion for sale. "Her leaders judge for a bribe, her priests teach for a price, and her prophets tell fortunes for money" (3:8). They had become skilled in doing evil and turned deceit into an art. They had not walked away from God. They had simply used him for their purposes, and no one had stopped them.

Micah goes on to say, "The faithful have been swept from the land; not one upright person remains" (v. 2). God does not disagree with Micah, and that is why this is not a call to repentance but an announcement of judgment. The whole society has become corrupt—right down to the roots. "Both hands are skilled in doing evil; the ruler demands gifts, the judge accepts bribes, the powerful dictate what they desire—they all conspire together. The best of them is like a brier, the most upright worse than a thorn hedge" (vv. 3–4).

The worst is when the corruption of leadership—the watchers—filters down to the last remains of trust in a society—neighbors and family. "Do not trust a neighbor; put no confidence in a friend. Even with the woman who lies in your embrace guard the words of your lips. For a son dishonors his father, a daughter rises up against her mother, a daughter-in-law against her mother-in-law—a man's enemies are the members of his own household" (vv. 5–6). The worst is when our leaders set such an example for the rest to follow. And when the family ties are gone, there is little hope for the rest.

So, we find Micah not calling the people to repentance. They are beyond that. Now he waits keeping watch for the Lord. But he waits in hope . . . and that is important.

What does he say? "Though I have fallen, I will rise. Though I sit in darkness, the LORD will be my light" (v. 8).

They have fallen not due to human frailty but to disobedience and deceit. The only cure for deceit and corruption is the truth. We are not merely frail creatures; we are broken. We are not disadvantaged; we are sinful by nature. All the progress in the world will not change that—not education or a better economy or universal healthcare or human ideas of justice. We are fallen. Micah goes on to say that because Israel has sinned—and he does not exclude himself from that—they will bear the wrath of God until God pleads their case and establishes them again.

To "bear" is the word *endure*, which can also mean "to accept responsibility for." We need to accept God's justified anger and accept the consequences of that. God's anger is not losing his temper. It has a purpose and a term. Jeremiah says that the Lord's anger will last until he has accomplished what he intends (Jer. 30:24). His anger is not a tantrum but a means to an end—and the end is always bringing people back to a right relationship with him.

Hebrews 12:7, 11 says, "Endure hardship as discipline; God is treating you as his children. . . . No discipline seems pleasant at the time, but painful. Later on, however, it produces a harvest of righteousness and peace for those who have been trained by it."

The ultimate purpose of his discipline is his glory—and that does not play well in a world caught up in self-improvement and self-interest where we believe even God's greatest interest is us. It's not. Listen to Ezekiel 36:22:

> "This is what the Sovereign LORD says, It is not for your
> sake, people of Israel, that I am going to do these things,
> but for the sake of my holy name, which you have pro-
> faned among the nations where you have gone."

God will be shown as holy through us, and that means doing whatever it takes to keep us from misrepresenting him. That was the sin of Israel that Micah was addressing. They had profaned the name of God by making a show of worship without the reality of righteousness. Worship was an experience but not one that demanded obedience.

But judgment is always in the context of hope. Human anger is always, at the end of the line, the last straw. God's anger is, in a sense, the *beginning* of something. But his anger has to clear away the sin before he can begin. That is the hope in which Micah waited. He knew the anger had to come before the rebuilding and he was waiting expectantly for it. There had to be consequences before there could be reconstruction.

God says he will rebuild what has been rubble. "The day for building your walls will come, the day for extending your boundaries" (Micah 7:11). Before the society is rebuilt, their hearts must be rebuilt.

Chuck Colson said shortly after becoming a Christian, "My greatest humiliation—being sent to prison—was the beginning of God's greatest use of my life."[16] Micah knew the humiliation had to come before the next chapter of

---

16 Charles Colson, *Loving God* (Grand Rapids: Zondervan, 1987), 35.

Israel's life. It wasn't resentment that made him sit and wait. It was knowing that God's wrath had to work before his rebuilding could begin.

That is what Micah waits for in hope instead of calling for repentance. There will be rubble for a time but then rebuilding. There will be desolation but then redemption. Darkness but then light.

But first there must be the outstretched arm of God that clears the ground for what is to come. That is our hope and God's place of beginning.

20

A HOUSE IN RUINS

Text: The Book of Haggai

We don't know much about the prophet Haggai other than he wrote during a time of international turmoil. Instability was everywhere. Kings had been deposed. Revolutions had overturned dynasties. Power was being shifted constantly and there were warring factions in every country surrounding Israel.

But in spite of that, Darius the King of Persia, decreed that a number of Jews could return to their homeland from exile in Babylon. Not many wanted to go back. In fact, it was probably less than 20,000 who left to return home. After seventy years of good treatment and finding a new way of life in the city of Babylon, most did not want to return to a country with very little to attract a new generation.

The book of Haggai was written sixteen years after the people had returned to Judah. When they first arrived, they were not welcomed home. For a variety of reasons, the Samaritans had no interest in the returning Jews rebuilding the temple or re-establishing themselves in the land. So, for years they kept the courts of Darius busy with lawsuits and objections that threw up one obstacle after another to the first Jewish settlers. They didn't take up arms against them. They just wore them down over time and made it more trouble than it was worth to rebuild the temple.

The returning Jews had not turned away from God but merely drifted into the course of least resistance and taking care of themselves. After all, they had learned to live without a temple for the entire time in exile—how important could it be? And that is when Haggai speaks:

> Then the word of the LORD came through the prophet Haggai: "Is it a time for you yourselves to be living in your paneled houses, while this house remains a ruin? . . . Give careful thought to your ways. You have planted much, but harvested little. You eat, but never have enough. You drink, but never have your fill. You put on clothes, but are not warm. You earn wages, only to put them in a purse with holes in it. . . .
> Give careful thought to your ways. Go up into the mountains and bring down timber and build my house, so that I may take pleasure in it and be honored," says the LORD. "You expected much, but see, it turned out to be little. What you brought home, I blew away. Why?" declares the LORD Almighty. "Because of my house, which remains a ruin, while each of you is busy with your own house." (Hag. 1:3–9)

"Give careful thought." This is not condemnation; it's not anger but more of a diagnostic question.

Perhaps you have allowed a temporary break or the path of least resistance to become a way of life. It's easy to do.

What are we busy building? Good things mostly. Yet, even in the good things there is a hunger that cannot be filled, a thirst that won't go away, a sense of never quite reaching our expectations. Those are signs from God and symptoms of a shrinking soul. Signals that we have become distracted from building the place where God dwells in our lives. Is God furious? No. He puts it to us in a way that makes us stop, put down what we are so busy doing, and give careful consideration to our lives.

Every time I go back to the book of Haggai, I am aware of the quiet voice of God asking me the same questions. What am I so busy doing that I have become distracted from the main thing?

What happened regularly in the physical temple?

- The reading of the Word

- Worship

- Prayer

- Fellowship

- Giving

- Serving and sacrifice

My own self-examination in these six areas gives me a reason to stop and judge what needs adjusting in my life—and it might be the same for you. Maybe we have become distracted by building other necessary and important things, and God is speaking to you through Haggai as he did to me.

Again, it is not condemnation but an invitation to self-examination.

But God is not completely satisfied with careful thought or introspection and self-examination. What does he say to them? "Go up into the mountains and bring down timber and build the house, so that I may take pleasure in it and be honored" (1:8).

Take the first step toward rebuilding. Find one tree and bring it down. Don't be overwhelmed. Don't try to do everything at once. Just start in the most obvious place.

It is important that God is with you in this endeavor because he wants to finish the work he began in you. It's easy to be discouraged when you feel you've let someone down but God does not withdraw or become cold and distant. His Spirit remains among us.

"Be strong, all you people of the land," declares the LORD, "and work. For I am with you," declares the LORD Almighty. "This is what I covenanted with you when you came out of Egypt. And my Spirit remains among you. Do not fear. . . . "From this day on . . . give careful thought to the day when the foundation of the LORD's temple was laid." (Hag. 2:4–5, 18)

And then what does he say?

"Give careful thought. . . . From this day on I will bless you" (v. 19).

Write today in your Bible if, like me, you have let good things distract you from building what God wants in your life. Write today's date in the margin if, like me, you have discovered that a temporary break has become a permanent habit of neglect.

Begin rebuilding today. Just pick one thing that you have put off or allowed to wither in your life. Start with one timber . . . but start.

21

RAISING THE BAR

Text: *The Book of Malachi*

This is a book about burdens—the burden of Malachi, the burden of leadership, and the burden of loving Israel in spite of their failures.

It has been about 100 years since Haggai's pronouncement to the returned Jews to rebuild the temple. The situation in Israel has changed. Not only have the people rebuilt the temple, there was also a time of spiritual recommitment under Ezra and Nehemiah. But, as almost always happened, when the leadership changed, the nation changed. The people have become careless and neglectful. While there was once a sense of anticipation for the imminent day of the Lord, there is now only skepticism, indifference, and a loss of hope. Some have even said cynically, "It is futile to serve God. What did we gain?" (Mal. 3:14). Others are discouraged by the amount of injustice that is overlooked—defrauding laborers of their wages, the oppression of widows and the fatherless, aliens being deprived of justice and calling the arrogant blessed.

The people have not run after other gods. They are not consumed by evil practices. They are simply disinterested in religion, disconnected from God, and discouraged by the behavior of the professional clergy.

Malachi speaks to the priests and the people both, but he seems to have a special burden for the priests as the spiritual leaders in the nation. It was a heavy responsibility to speak to priests and convict them—not just to accuse them or pick them apart. Malachi is not a bomb thrower but one who is genuinely committed to them.

This is, in some ways, a private letter to the priests. It is honest and cuts to the heart of the issues. But it begins with "'I have loved you,' says the LORD" (1:1). God's discipline always begins with that and it is that alone that allows us to bear what follows.

They respond with "How have you loved us?" That tells you how deep the problem is. They no longer believe they are loved by God. They are still priests, but they have lost their way. I am not saying that pastors who question God's love are not fit for ministry. I suspect in almost every pastor's heart there have been questions about God's love for them more than once. Ministry is sometimes dark and depressing.

I have heard pastors say that they have become professional pretenders. They have to keep up appearances for the church, but they stopped believing God loved them years ago. The priests in Malachi have lost all sense of the love of God. If the priests no longer believe in God's love, then what would be the effect on the people?

What is even worse is what we read in 1:13: "And you say, 'What a burden!' And you sniff at it contemptuously." They are not only doubtful of the love of God but embarrassed by their work and the people they are with.

And then God says, "It is you priests who show contempt for my name" (1:6). And they respond, "How have we defiled you?" (v. 7). I think one of the greatest marks of weak leaders is having low expectations for people. It is a way of despising the followers and excusing themselves. It's a vicious circle—they disappoint you, and you disappoint them in return.

But God has no hesitation in asking for our best. Have you ever been in a situation where only your best was accepted? It was probably your most demanding teacher, a coach, or a project team leader. What was the effect on you and the others? It was probably hard but exhilarating. Maybe there were times in the middle when you thought you would fail but then you overcame the obstacles. Had you not been challenged by someone or some situation, you would have lost a rare opportunity.

On the other hand, what is it like to work in an environment of low expectations? We did the minimum to get by and no one complained or wanted anything different. It killed the spirit. It attacked our ambition and enthusiasm.

Alexander Pope puts it this way, "Blessed is he who expects nothing, for he shall never be disappointed."

Bad leadership always robs people of the joy of sacrifice and accomplishment. Demanding the best of people IS a weight. It IS a burden. It IS a heavy responsibility and it would be far easier to give up and be contemptuous of them.

There are times when the church robs their people of the reward of giving their best by having low expectations of them. We give services for free and ask hardly anything in return. The more programs we offer, the less commitment we experience. We have stopped asking people for sacrifice, and the church is in a constant search for more ways to attract people who are always wanting more for less.

But this is not all the fault of the priests, is it? We are often the ones who are demanding more but only on our terms. God says through Malachi, "Oh, that one of you would shut the temple doors, so that you would not light useless fires on my altar!" (1:10). What might we do if all the free services, inspiring music, teaching, and conveniences went away temporarily? Would we find ourselves fading spiritually or might we actually grow? The power of the church is not a buffet of options for customers. The power of the church has always been sacrifice.

The people of Israel had grown disinterested in religion unless it served them. They had become impatient and tired of waiting for God to do more special things for them. They had fallen asleep spiritually and lost their zeal for God.

How do we stay faithful when things are not exciting? How much more do we need to believe God loves us? It is not so much suffering that kills our spirit as it is the mundane.

Jesus often used the image of waiting in his parables. In Luke 19 the people thought the kingdom was coming soon, and Jesus tells them the story of the man who went away to a distant country but did not say when he would be back. Some did well and some did not. Or in Luke 20 he tells the story of the man who planted a vineyard and went away for a long time. While he was gone the tenants revolted. In Matthew 25 Jesus uses the parable of the ten virgins when the bridegroom was a long time in coming and they all fell asleep. Or, finally, the disciples in Gethsemane who fall asleep three times while waiting for Jesus to pray.

Our life is measured by how well we wait. And that may be OUR burden. How do we live with expectancy and not fall into unfaithfulness or sleep? How do we manage to fulfill what Eugene Peterson calls the "long obedience in the same direction" while we wait? How do we, as Paul said, live in hope of the not yet seen but keep our eyes focused on what will be even though it is not yet (Rom. 8:24–25)? I think that is the mark of maturity that is so difficult to master—to wait and not lose heart or fall asleep.

22

A LATE BLOOMER

Text: *The Gospel of Mark; Acts 15*

Every time I read the break-up story of John Mark, Paul, and Barnabas in Acts 15, I am surprised by the ending. I am not going to spoil it for those of you who have never read it all the way through to the end, but this is one of the best illustrations I know of what happens when we read Scripture in snippets and verses. We miss the bigger picture. We miss the details of a life that so influenced the formation of not only the early church but the Church universal. However, you would never know it from just reading this account:

> Some time later Paul said to Barnabas, "Let us go back and visit the believers in all the towns where we preached the word of the Lord and see how they are doing." Barnabas wanted to take John, also called Mark, with them, but Paul did not think it wise to take him, because he had deserted them in Pamphylia and had not continued with them in the work. They had such a sharp disagreement that they parted company. Barnabas took Mark and sailed for Cyprus, but Paul chose Silas and left. (vv. 36–40)

John Mark has an interesting story—especially for early failures, late bloomers, and parents of late bloomers.

His mother, Mary, was wealthy and influential. Her house was the central meeting place for the early church. It's likely that it was her upper room that was the setting of the Last Supper as well as the place the disciples were gathered when Jesus first appeared to them after the resurrection. As a young man, he was surrounded by the apostles and heroes of the movement. He had access to relationships and advantages that were rare.

But . . . he is more than likely the young man who ran out of Gethsemane rather than be arrested with Jesus. He flees the early persecution of the church and goes to Antioch.

His cousin Barnabas is influential and powerful and secures him a place with him and Paul on the first missionary journey. It's one of the first unpaid internships and just another example of how privileged John Mark was as a young man.

But he leaves them in Pamphylia because the work is too hard and goes back home to Jerusalem. In doing so, he misses all the hardships and successes of that first journey. Still, he had to listen to all of the stories at the Council when they returned several years later. You can imagine how uncomfortable that must have been knowing he had dropped out and run home, feeling like a failure.

J. K. Rowling, the author of the Harry Potter series, was the commencement speaker for Harvard in 2008 and part of her address was on the value of failure:

> A mere seven years after my graduation day, I had failed on an epic scale. An exceptionally short-lived marriage had imploded, and I was jobless, a lone parent, and as poor as it is possible to be in modern Britain, without being homeless. . . . So why do I talk about the benefits of failure? Simply because failure meant a stripping away of the inessential. I stopped pretending to myself that I was anything other than what I was, and began to direct all my energy into finishing the only work that mattered to me. Had I really succeeded at anything else,

I might never have found the determination to succeed in the one arena I believed I truly belonged. I was set free, because my greatest fear had been realised, and I was still alive, and I still had a daughter whom I adored, and I had an old typewriter and a big idea. And so rock bottom became the solid foundation on which I rebuilt my life.[17]

After Barnabas and Paul split over John Mark, he goes to Cyprus with Barnabas. For Paul, John Mark was clearly a deserter. Paul didn't want anyone with him who could not live up to his expectations. Barnabas, however, saw the potential in people. After all, he was the one who brought the brash new convert Saul to the apostles and vouched for him. This was no mild disagreement for Paul and Barnabas. It was a fight that split them from each other for the rest of their lives. They never see each other again.

After Barnabas's stoning in Cyprus in AD 61, we lose track of John Mark for almost ten years. Given his pattern of running and quitting, we would not expect much of him. He would just fade away and self-destruct—a child of privilege with unused potential.

Then ten years later, Paul says to Timothy, "Get Mark and bring him with you because he is helpful to me in my ministry. . . . everyone deserted me" (2 Tim. 4:11, 16).

What changed?

In those silent years, Mark had attached himself to the one person in his life—Peter—who could relate completely to a young man who had deserted, failed, and betrayed. In Peter, John Mark finds a father, a fellow sinner, and a friend. But something else happened. He began to write down Peter's recollections of Jesus and, in doing so, he was changed.

---

17   The full commencement speech can be found at https://www.youtube.com/watch?v=UibfDUPJAEU.

- John Mark didn't become good at something until later in life—a late bloomer.

- John Mark needed a patron—someone who had the patience and empathy to believe in him.

- John Mark needed someone to give him a task to accomplish.

There are two major characteristics of the Gospel of Mark: First, we know more about Peter's flaws than any other book. His fears, his denial of Jesus, and his desertion of the disciples. Second, we see Jesus primarily as a man of action, not words. He has authority and strength. He is a man of energy, courage, and command. He is the Lion of Judah.

What did Mark discover as he wrote the gospel? He discovered himself and a Jesus that changed his life. Peter's flaws were the same as his, and Peter's Christ became his.

So, what is the rest of the story?

Mark is sent by Peter to Alexandria to become the first bishop of the Church in Egypt. He is the founder of the Coptic (Greek for "Egypt") Church, of which there are about 12 million Coptic Christians there today. In AD 68 he is martyred by being dragged for two days behind a horse until all of his skin is removed. Many years later it is said that the founders of Venice, Italy, wanted a saint's relics, so they stole Mark's head and took it back to Venice. There it became the most precious relic of one of the most famous cathedrals in the world—St. Mark's—and he became the patron saint of the city of Venice.

But here is what I find interesting—something we could have not predicted when we first met him. The early church gave him the symbol of the winged lion, and it is the flag of Venice still today. It is a symbol of power, authority, and strength. On the flag, the lion personifies the voice of John the Baptist in the introduction of the Gospel. The wings are from Ezekiel 1:10. The lion holds the scroll because he is the author of the earliest gospel and the inscription reads, "Peace to thee, Mark, my evangelist." The boy who ran away became a lion—just like Jesus the Lion of Judah in his Gospel.

Don't ever count anyone out. God doesn't. We all will have a flag one day that will symbolize who we are and what we have stood for. In Mark we can celebrate the redeeming of early mistakes, the forgiveness of failure, and God's ability to turn young, spoiled boys into men with hearts of lions.

23

JUST YOU WAIT . . .

Text: Mark 9

I think every retreat I attended concluded with the warning that when returning from a mountaintop experience, we were likely to face the valley of reality and frustration. William Barclay said, "The solitude is not meant to make us solitary. It is meant to make us better able to meet and cope with the demands of everyday life."[18]

This is especially true for Jesus and the three disciples in Mark 9 as they have just experienced the transfiguration—the revelation of God himself. Jesus returns to find everyone arguing about a boy with an evil spirit. While Peter, James, and John are still living off the fumes of a supernatural experience, Jesus has to deal with the internal squabbling between his disciples and the scribes. The scribes were professionals at arguing and debating, being lawyers who spent their lives studying and interpreting the Law for the people. I suspect the disciples were on the ropes in front of the people by the time Jesus shows up. Though the scribes were very knowledgeable, they had become narrow, elitist, and focused on academic squabbles. It's the great danger of knowledge. It feeds pride and the sense of being special.

---

18   William Barclay, *The Gospel of Mark* (Daily Study Bible) (Louisville: Westminster John Knox Press, 1975), 214–15.

My guess is they were not arguing with the disciples about their failure to heal the boy. I doubt they had an interest in the boy at all. What was probably more important to them was settling the question posed to Jesus in John 9:2: "Who sinned, this man or his parents, that he was born blind?" The health of the boy was secondary to debating to see who was right. If the boy had been healed by the disciples, the scribes would lose. If the boy was not healed, it didn't matter because it was the argument that was most interesting to them. Who sinned? Who is to blame? The boy and the father were forgotten. It's not unlike some of our debates today.

Jesus asks, "What are you arguing with them about?" (Mark 9:16). He continues: "You unbelieving generation . . . how long shall I stay with you? How long shall I put up with you?" I think he is addressing not the father but the scribes and the disciples.

What makes for an unbelieving generation?

- The pride of knowledge makes us less interested in trust.

- An ever-increasing skepticism about everyone and everything.

- Our own experiences in the world. Our own disappointments and misgivings.

- Our fear of being wrong and choosing the losing side.

- Being constantly bombarded with people arguing their position. We are weary of persuasion.

All of these things together create an unbelieving generation, and it is as true today as it was then. There was no faith in God, only in their traditions and arguments.

Yet, Jesus's response is not to focus on their faithlessness but to turn to the father and say "Bring the boy to me" (v. 19). The demon has been with him since childhood and it was intent on taking his life. While what is described here would be diagnosed as epilepsy today, there are still some demons that start off in our lives as tendencies when we are young, become habits, and when they work their way into our nature, they become spirits that control us. A sharp tongue becomes a spirit of sarcasm. Doubt become a spirit of worry. The intention of such spirits is always the same—to steal life and to kill the best in us.

Jesus takes the boy and his father off to the side and asks questions. He is totally focused on the father and the boy apart from the crowd. Jesus had the ability to give himself completely to whoever he was with. Henri Nouwen called it the "ministry of presence." Jesus's questions are not diagnostic but one of genuine interest. "How long has he been like this?" It was not "what's his problem?" but more like "tell me about the boy."

But, like his encounter with Jairus whose son is desperately ill or with Lazarus who dies because Jesus waits to come, there is a delay. The boy is on the ground, the father is desperate, and Jesus is asking questions. He is not controlled by the urgent even when it looks like he is pushing people to their breaking point which he sometimes does. He pushes them beyond themselves. He waits.

In some ways, this explains his comment that "this kind can come out only by prayer" (v. 29) because it is a discipline of prayer that gives you the ability and the faith to wait. We want to rush in and fix things for everyone. We don't know how to wait. We don't have the confidence to wait. I think God was after more than healing the boy. I think he was after the father as well . . . and that required waiting.

The desperate father acknowledges his belief and yet begs Jesus to help him with his unbelief (v. 24). It is this transparent, two-layer aspect of faith that we all feel at times. "I do, but I need help with the part I don't."

After the boy has been healed, the disciples are still grumbling about why they had failed. I think part of the answer is found in what happens next. What were they continuing to argue about? Was it the boy and his father? No, it was who among them was the greatest (vv. 33–37). I believe it is the same pride and scrambling for recognition that keeps us from understanding what Jesus is after in our lives.

Those who have lost children and believe they have died or remained sick due to some sin of the parent may read this account and think their faith was lacking. If only they had prayed more. If only they had believed more. That is why I don't think this story is about finding a formula for great faith—that would be cruel. It was about God's encounter with a particular person, not a universal application. So, I don't want anyone in a similar situation thinking they just need to have more faith and God will heal their child or their spouse or loved one. It's not a one-size-fits-all story.

The common thread we can glean from the story is how those of us with knowledge overlook people and become engaged in meaningless disputes. It is about our losing our connection with Christ in our desire for greatness and position and esteem. It is about our slipping into faithlessness and disbelief. I cannot explain why some are healed and some are not. I do not trust in formulas and lists of magic practices, but I can say with Paul, "I know whom I have believed, and am convinced that he is able to guard what I have entrusted to him until that day" (2 Tim. 1:12).

24

ADAPT OR DIE

| Text: Luke 5 |

I have often questioned the phrase, "What Would Jesus Do?" First, he had abilities to do things we do not. He could walk on water, heal the sick, give sight to the blind, raise the dead, and heal the paralyzed. As well, it is sometimes difficult to predict what Jesus would do. We look for a tight pattern and we are almost always surprised. Sometimes he responds to crowds and sometimes he gets away from them. Sometimes he heals directly and other times he uses a process like mud on the eyes or even a second touch. Sometimes he warns people not to say anything and other times he does not. He is what we would call inconsistent and unpredictable and trying to pin him down to one response for every situation and person is impossible.

But one thing is constant—the people come to him in droves from everywhere. We see that in Luke 4 and 5. He heals many in Peter's hometown of Capernaum—including his mother-in-law—and then early the next morning Jesus escapes the crowds, and the disciples have to come looking for him. He heals a leper and then sends him away to the priest with a strong warning to not tell anyone.

Crowds form around a few motivations—anxiety, fear, anger, or hope. The crowds in the early days formed around hope. For now, the scribes, lawyers, Pharisees, and Sadducees sit by, but it won't be long before they turn the crowds against Jesus.

Our focus is on one special healing—and the friends who made it happen:

> One day Jesus was teaching, and Pharisees and teachers of the law were sitting there. They had come from every village of Galilee and from Judea and Jerusalem. And the power of the Lord was with Jesus to heal the sick. Some men came carrying a paralyzed man in a mat and tried to take him into the house to lay before Jesus. When they could not find a way to do this because of the crowd, they went up on the roof and lowered him on his mat through the tiles into the middle of the crowd, right in front of Jesus. (Luke 5:17–19)

These are unusual friends. I would like to have them on my side. They are resourceful, aggressive, and maybe even obnoxious about pushing their way to the roof. Had I been Jesus, I would have been upset with them for tearing up someone's property and getting ahead of everyone else in line. How does Jesus respond? He has not only patience for them but uses them as an example for others. There are other places in the Gospels where Jesus seems to favor people like this:

- The persistent widow who will not stop pestering the judge (Luke 18:1–8)

- The wicked steward whose bad behavior is not condemned but accepted (Luke 16:1–13)

- The beggar who shouts until he gets the attention of Jesus (Mark 10:46–49)

- The woman who grabs at the hem of his robe (Matt. 9:18–26)

Sometimes we are not pushy enough with God. Yes, we plead and petition, but we do not push. Moses complains about his assignment to deliver the people. David tells God that he needs to protect his own reputation. He almost preaches to God about what he needs to do. Jeremiah argues with God about why the wicked prosper. They all push back. It is not ingratitude or insolence but being so secure with God that they can speak openly.

We are, I think, afraid to be real. We think God is too fragile or is unwilling to listen to what we really want to say. So, we cover up our true feelings of anger, disappointment, and complaint. God knows our thoughts already, and he can handle our questions and our pushiness.

Luke goes on to say, "When Jesus saw their faith [referring to the friends of the paralyzed man], he said, "Friend, your sins are forgiven" (v. 20).

Of course, the question in the minds of the Pharisees and the teachers is: "Who is this fellow who speaks blasphemy? Who can forgive sins but God alone?" (v. 21). After thousands of years I think the question is the same. How do we respond to people who claim things that go against everything we believe to be true and that we have been taught since childhood? For us, it may be the inerrancy of Scripture; the way to God is through Jesus alone; the marriage of one man and one woman. Where is the balance between blind and unquestioning tradition and outright heresy?

There is one thing that is common to us all. Once we have created a monopoly on something, we are reluctant to let it go. We don't like it when someone breaks up our hold on things—and that is what Jesus was doing. He was saying the monopoly on forgiveness is over.

In some ways, the Western world is facing the same in the growth of Christianity. For many of us, we so identify with our Christian history and institutions that we fail to realize where the church is growing and the changes it is experiencing. The Christian world we have known for so long—the world of Europe and America—is fast becoming the minority in the church. It will take time but the center of Christianity has already shifted. We can adapt or disappear.

In the mid-2010s, astronomical growth resulted in an estimated 614 million Pentecostals, charismatics, and neo-charismatics, according to the Center for the Study of Global Christianity at Gordon-Conwell Theological Seminary. This surge is expected to increase to 797 million by 2025. No longer is it largely the work of "white" missions. The half a billion Pentecostal/charismatics are now predominantly Africans, Latin Americans, and Asians.[19]

The world church is becoming black and brown—and some of us are not going to be comfortable with that. We are going to huddle and wish for the good old days when the church looked like us.

By forgiving sins, Jesus was not only threatening the way things had been and the people who had been in charge, but he was threatening the most important power that God held—the power of forgiveness. Sometimes our fallback for the inability to adapt is to call it blasphemy. Then Jesus took it a step further. Not only did he heal and forgive sins, but he put the power of faith into the hands of his friends. The paralytic may not have had any faith at all, but his friends did. Sometimes what we are facing is too much, and that is when friends step in with faith that makes up for our lacking. That is when we need pushy friends.

God in Christ has delegated power to believers. We don't need priests or professionals to tell us we are forgiven by God. We can speak God's forgiveness into the lives of other people.

Maybe some of you need to be carried by the faith of your friends because you are paralyzed or hopeless or out of belief. Let them do it.

There might be people tearing holes in your roof, interrupting you, being inconvenient and demanding, in order to get your attention. Be patient and kind.

This week you are going to be distressed by some of the changes going on in the world. Not all of them are blasphemy and some of them are there to stretch you. Be open.

---

19 Information gleaned from "Christianity 2010: A View from the New *Atlas of Christianity*," http://www.internationalbulletin.org/issues/2010-01/2010-01-029-johnson.pdf.

25

THE SNARE FOR SIN

Text: John 19

After an earthquake, scientists work to find both the epicenter and the hypocenter. The epicenter is the point on the earth's surface vertically above the initial quake. The actual quake begins deep below the epicenter in what is called the hypocenter. It is the point in the crust of the earth where the rupture actually occurs. The epicenter is the visible evidence of the hypocenter.

In the crucifixion, we have both. The quake of the victory over sin and death is located here—at the cross. You could say X marks the spot. It is here that the whole sinful order of the world is fractured from deep within and only visible because of the cross. Forever after we can point to a time and place that everything shifted.

The early church did not focus, as we do today, on the excruciating pain and degradation of the process. Mark was not writing a screenplay. He was not thinking about Mel Gibson's dwelling on the physical abuse and agony of the beatings, bloody excesses, and torture of being crucified. Mark did not have to create shock value or stimulate the senses to get his readers to feel the pain because the pain was not central to the message.

The focus in Scripture is not on the gruesome death but on the controlled power of Jesus in the face of such sin. We emphasize what they did to him which minimizes his being in charge of everything. Our well-intentioned songs say, "I'm the one to blame. I caused all his pain," yet we have substituted grisly and manipulated emotions for gratitude . . . and missed the point. He chose to die in a particular way at a specific time. Christ did not die because I or you put him to death. He died to reverse the fall of Adam and the inheritance of the sin nature. He died that I might live and that the world might be reconciled to God through his death—"God made him who had no sin to be sin for us, so that in him we might become the righteousness of God" (2 Cor. 5:21).

Again, Jesus is not a victim. He predicts his death several times so it is not a surprise. He is not a teacher caught up in a crossfire of politics and religion. He is in charge of the whole process. Jesus remained silent because a single word, a miracle, a sign, an argument would have disrupted the intentional purpose. He came to be offered as a sacrifice and not a victim, a martyr, or a misunderstood hero. Peter says in Acts 2:23: "This man was handed over to you by God's deliberate plan and foreknowledge." In other words, this was not a plot against Jesus but a plot designed by him.

But to focus only on the life or death of Jesus is to distort the gospel. Paul's focus is not on Jesus's biography or even his teachings . . . but on his role as the perfect. Paul quotes Moses, Abraham and the Psalms far more than he quotes Jesus. Paul does not teach in parables or even reminisce about Jesus. He never asks, "What would Jesus do?" Paul virtually ignores Jesus's earthly life because of the greater and essential work of Jesus as the Christ—the reconciler.

I know that talking about the blood of Christ is often uncomfortable. For many years it was an obstacle for me. I not only had a great fear of blood itself, but the whole issue was distasteful and off-putting. I wanted the gospel but I wanted it cleaned up. I would skip church when I knew the worship leader was going to have us sing what he called "blood medleys." It sounded grisly—like some Stephen King novel.

Nothing but the Blood
Oh! precious is the flow
That makes me white as snow;

No other fount I know,
Nothing but the blood of Jesus.

Power in the Blood
Would you be whiter, much whiter than snow?
There's pow'r in the blood, pow'r in the blood;
Sin-stains are lost in its life-giving flow;
There's wonderful pow'r in the blood.

There Is a Fountain Filled with Blood
There is a fountain filled with blood drawn from Emmanuel's veins;
And sinners plunged beneath that flood lose all their guilty stains.

No wonder people called it "that bloody religion." It was . . . and it is.

We want God to be something other than what he reveals himself to be. We want to excuse or explain the more barbaric and violent parts of his behavior. How can we market a loving and kind God to the world if he demands blood? The Greek in us wants philosophy, order, intellectual stimulation, and reason. A safe and sensible God we can introduce to friends without any reservations or embarrassment.

However, if we are to understand what it means to be at peace with God, we need to understand the blood. There are four ways:

1. The blood is our protection (read Exod. 12:7–13).

2. The blood is the basis of the covenant with Israel (read Exod. 24:3–8).

3. The blood is a requirement for atonement (read Lev. 16:15–22).

4. The blood is the requirement for peace with God (read Eph. 2:13 and Col. 1:20).

Our understanding and accepting the requirement of the blood of Jesus is essential because it is the heart of how we are reconciled with God. A bloodless Christianity is powerless. What does Paul say in 1 Corinthians 1:17: "For Christ did not send me to baptize, but to preach the gospel—not with wisdom and eloquence, lest the cross of Christ be emptied of its power."

We want a less bloody, less violent, and more thoughtful religion. No more blood medleys. No fountains filled with it or sinners plunged beneath it. It's okay to have a man give up his life for us, but let's downplay the blood. However, as Paul says, we are grafted on to the root and without the root, we will die (Rom. 11:11–34). We cannot separate ourselves from our Jewish roots, and at the core of Judaism is blood and sacrifice and atonement for a holy God. If we do, all that is left are just stories about Jesus. Christianity without Jewish roots eliminates Creation, the Fall, the covenant with Abraham, the Law, the Messiah, and the people of God. Christianity without talking about blood is a rootless, immaterial, and meaningless philosophy. It is a distorted religion of cheap grace and false love.

The cross is the tool by which the blood was shed. The cross is where X marks the spot. The cross was the ingenious trap God laid for sin. The cross is God's invitation to reconciliation with the world.

What can wash away our sins? What can make us whole again? Truly, there is nothing but the blood.

26

TEN PERFECT DAYS

Text: Acts 2

We see the coming of the Holy Spirit at Pentecost in Acts 2. It's difficult to understand the meaning of Pentecost (Greek for 50th day) unless we look first at the chapter that precedes it. What is the context of the 50th day?

While there were a number of feasts and festivals in the life of Jews, there were three main solemn feasts in Jewish life for which every adult male was required to make the trip to Jerusalem:

1. Passover

2. The Feast of Weeks (Pentecost) seven weeks later

3. The Feast of Tabernacles in the fall

To each of them was attached an offering of firstfruits related to the season:

1. barley for Passover

2. two loaves of bread for the Feast of Weeks (Pentecost)

3. olives and grapes for the Feast of Tabernacles

Pentecost was also a special kind of feast in that it included everyone. Look at Deuteronomy 16:9–10: "Count off seven weeks from the time you begin to put the sickle to the standing grain. Then celebrate the Festival of Weeks to the LORD your God by giving a freewill offering in proportion to the blessings the LORD your God has given you."

The main point in our text is taken from an event that followed two other events. The first was Passover (the crucifixion and resurrection of Jesus) followed by his being with the disciples and others for forty days before his ascension into heaven. That means Pentecost came fifty days after his resurrection and ten days after the ascension.

Before Jesus ascended, the disciples questioned him: "Lord, are you going to restore the kingdom to Israel?" (Acts 1:6). It would have been natural to see the connection between his resurrection and the restoration of King David's kingdom. In ten days, Pentecost, they would celebrate not only the Feast of Weeks, but it was also the day when all of Israel remembered the death of King David. It is called a *yahrzeit* and it means an annual celebration of the life of an important person. No one could have been more important to those who were looking for the restoration of the former kingdom.

They still had no idea what Jesus had in mind. For them, like for some of us, we live in hopes of restoring kingdoms—of making things the way they used to be. No one wants kingdoms restored unless they were in charge of the kingdom. No one wanted the exile of Babylon or the bondage of Egypt restored. They wanted the return of the time they had been told about and what they thought they had been promised. In a sense, Pentecost is an answer to their question about the restoration of the kingdom. We'll see how in a minute.

For ten days the early church functioned almost perfectly as an organization, but they lacked the one thing they needed to fulfill their purpose—*the power to be witnesses.*

The defining work of the church is not prayer or attendance growth or good deeds or preaching or fellowship. It's not spotless lives or sacrificial service. These things are good but not adequate. The work of the church—to be witnesses (literally *martyrs* in Greek)—only gets done through the supernatural power of the Holy Spirit. My father would say there are three types of churches: badly run human institutions; well-run human institutions; and Spirit-led congregations.

And witnesses to what? They were not witnesses to what God had done for them but what God had done in Jesus—the resurrection of the dead! Five times in the book of Acts they describe what they are witnesses to: Acts 2:32; 3:15; 4:20; 5:30; and 10:40. Each time they say essentially, "God raised Jesus from the dead and we are witnesses."

Pentecost is not about restoring a kingdom. It is redefining the Feast of Weeks from a Jewish observance to a global mission. Pentecost marked the beginning of the harvest—not planting. It marked celebrating what God has already done—not what we are doing. Too often we make the assumption that God is not present until we bring him.

As I've said before, there are two phrases I hesitate to use. First, "What would Jesus do?" and second, "Find out where God is moving and join him there." Where is God *not* moving? Where is God *not* planting? Yes, belief comes by preaching, but it is more like announcing and less like arm-twisting. It is not pleading or frightening or brow-beating. It is recognizing that there are no methods we can devise that will produce the unique work of the Holy Spirit. We are witnesses to what God has already done in Jesus.

But there was something else about Pentecost or the Feast of Weeks. It was the one time a year when Jews recognized the most important event in their history: the giving of the Law to Moses. Yes, the rescue from Egypt was central, but it was the giving of the Law that created their identity as a special people set aside for a holy purpose.

So, what does it mean then to be a Pentecostal church? It doesn't mean what we have made it to be, does it?

- It's not just a church that emphasizes certain gifts of the Spirit but a church that fulfills the original purpose of Pentecost—to be a witness to the resurrection of Christ.

- It is a diverse church. It celebrates the destruction of barriers and distinctions.

- It is a church that is not interested in restoring a former kingdom or creating a Christian kingdom here on earth.

- It is a church that includes the poor, the stranger, the widow, and the orphan. It takes seriously its responsibility to these.

- It is a church grateful for what God has done and does not make itself the center of the story.

- It is a church that recognizes it can be a growing and successful church, yet still lack one important thing—the power to be a witness to the resurrection of Jesus and a light in a dark world.

Jesus fulfilled the original purpose of all of these festivals—especially Pentecost. Instead of the giving of the Law, it became the giving of the Spirit. He did not create something out of nothing. Instead, he took something they all understood and redefined it—totally. For some, he stretched it beyond all recognition and they could not handle it. In fact, it might have been easier to start new and throw everything out. But he didn't. Jesus was the fulfilment of the Old Testament promise, and he used Jewish traditions to bring about God's plan for the whole world.

27

THREE RULES OF FREEDOM

Text: Acts 15

As Luke tells us, after Paul's conversion he spends two years in Arabia and then a year in Damascus and Tarsus before Barnabas is sent to look for him and bring him to Antioch where they spend a year teaching until they are commissioned as missionaries. Together, they spend the next ten years traveling and planting churches. They periodically return to Antioch to give reports of their hardships and their success. Throughout those ten years Paul has run-ins and struggles with Jewish believers (the Judaizers) who insist that new believers be circumcised and follow the dietary laws. So, the first major church council is convened in Jerusalem with the leaders of the church—James and Peter—to decide the issue. Paul and Barnabas travel to Jerusalem to represent the young churches and make their case for Gentiles not being required to convert to Judaism.

In a way, it's a surprise they were able to go for fourteen years before dealing with this issue—especially as strongly it was felt by some that being a follower of Jesus required following the Law. It had to come to a head sooner or later.

Acts 15:7–11 describes Peter's response to the Council:

> "Brothers, you know that some time ago God made a choice among you that the Gentiles might hear from

my lips the message of the gospel and believe. God, who knows the heart, showed that he accepted them by giving the Holy Spirit to them, just as he did to us. He did not discriminate between us and them, for he purified their hearts by faith. Now then, why do you try to test God by putting on the necks of Gentiles a yoke that neither we nor our ancestors have been able to bear? No! We believe it is through the grace of our Lord Jesus that we are saved, just as they are."

James speaks up as well: "It is my judgment, therefore, that we should not make it difficult for the Gentiles who are turning to God. Instead we should write to them, telling them to abstain from food polluted by idols, from sexual immorality, from the meat of strangled animals and from blood" (vv. 19–20).

Why only those three rules? Why not Sabbath or tithing? Why not insist they at least obey the Ten Commandments? There were hundreds of rules from which to choose and they specifically chose these three: abstain from food sacrificed to idols, from blood and meat of strangled animals (kosher), and from sexual immorality. There must have been good reason to be so specific.

The Council were concerned that the Gentiles would get unhooked from Judaism and lose themselves in the spirit of the age, that they would be absorbed back into the culture from which they came. On their own, there was nothing to separate them, and these three would do that. It would not require them to become Jews but it would, if obeyed, make them distinct. I think they were looking ahead from a particular tradition realizing they were becoming larger and more diverse than a small sect of Jewish believers. They were figuring out how to deal with growth and change as best they could. They did not want to lose their traditions but they did not want to send the Gentiles off with no link to their roots.

Think of it this way—they were giving the new believers "luggage" for the journey. They were not loading them down with a burden. They were giving them some basic things they would need for the future.

I am not sure we could have given as much latitude as the Council did (even though two of three rules are so outdated we don't even think about them as being relevant). Would we be as secure as they were, especially if we had to reduce the non-negotiables to just three things? What would we choose? What would we say are the absolutes and the core values about our faith without which we would lose our identity? That's probably harder to do than we realize.

Yet, without focus on the fewest core principles, you will begin to add regulations to make sure people obey. You end up with what we have now—lack of trust in the principles, thus creating thousands of pages of legalistic rules.

What then are the underlying principles of these three observances? What is packed in the luggage for them?

1. The temptation of idols is hard to resist. They are attractive and they seduce slowly and unnoticeably. So, we need something tangible that reminds us of how dangerous and subtle they are. Don't get too familiar with people who worship idols.

2. In a world that is so caught up in lust, there is a place for purity. Every good thing—not just sex—can become an object of a craving desire.

3. While those early Christians lived in places where rulers had absolutely no regard for life and turned sacrifice into sport, the Christians were to recognize that life belongs to God and is entrusted to us.

What is the gift the Council is giving to these Greek believers? I like to think about it as a trail of crumbs they will have to find their way home if they get lost. It was the DNA for true religion they could use to re-create what is extinguished. They were a life preserver for the deep waters that would keep them from drowning in the flood that surrounded and, at times, overwhelmed.

But times and cultures change. It may be the church today requires different advice to serve as bread crumbs, DNA and life jackets. Maybe we need to convene a new Council and pick different requirements. Meat offered to idols and strangled animals are not a problem, are they? We still need reminding daily even if the rituals are different. We still need some basics:

- There is only one God and everything else is weightless and empty.
- Moral purity is essential and it is not just a personal choice—immorality corrupts the whole church.
- Life is precious and it belongs to God.

Maybe we need a new Council today that will not burden new believers and those who are turning to God with our rules and regulations. Maybe it is not necessary to be a "traditional Christian" to turn to God. Converts can love Christ without the labels and burdens we might impose on them. There is a great shift going on now. The center of the church is shifting from the West to the South. People are calling themselves Christ-followers and not Christians because Christian now connotes a political agenda. People are leaving institutions and joining movements. People are leaving traditional churches and hoping to be more in touch with the Spirit than the structure. How will we respond?

I know how Paul responded to the Council when he compared his and Barnabas's ministry to the Gentiles with the equally important work of Peter with the Jewish believers: "James, [Peter] and John, those esteemed as pillars, gave me and Barnabas the right hand of fellowship when they recognized the grace given to me. They agreed that we should go to the Gentiles, and they to the circumcised. All they asked was that we should continue to remember the poor, the very thing I had been eager to do all along" (Gal. 2:9–10)).

Did you catch that?—"continue to remember the poor . . ." What happened to the other three? While the intent of the Council leaders had been good, it would have eventually stifled the growth of the church. For Paul, the one requirement above all others was the same as Jesus had left the disciples. *Love one another.* Sacrifice for each other. Practice humility and self-control not for simply for personal growth but for the maturity of the church. For Paul, the only DNA was the work and indwelling of the Holy Spirit—not a set of policies and procedures.

Then what are the three requirements Paul packs in our luggage for the journey?

1. Take care of each other: "Carry each other's burdens" (Gal. 6:2).

2. Submit to one another: "In humility value others above yourselves" (Phil. 2:3).

3. Your life is not your own: "You were bought at a price" (1 Cor. 7:23).

I know, it is much easier to follow food laws and well-defined regulations. That way we know who is in and who is out. We know where we stand and how we are doing. But then Paul comes along and says, "The entire law is fulfilled in keeping this one command: 'Love your neighbor as yourself'" (5:14). But that is what makes the church supernatural. It is the impossible command that can only be done through the power of the Holy Spirit. Everything else—growth, miracles, organization, power, influence—we can do on our own, but one thing we are lacking. It is that one thing alone that makes us the church—we love one another.

28

FAILURE IS NOT FATAL

Text: Acts 16

It's easy to read Paul's letter to the church at Philippi and not connect it to the people to whom he wrote. The words are so lovely. The scope of the theology is extraordinary, and the depth of his emotion and attachment to them has inspired millions of people for thousands of years. Other than 1 Corinthians 13, there is likely no passage that surpasses Philippians 2 in describing the character and qualities of Christian love. These must have been unusual people—probably the most unusual mix of people in the New Testament—to have stirred such feelings in Paul and caused him to write them from a Roman prison a long twelve years after he first met them.

First, there was Lydia. She led a discussion and prayer group by the river on the Sabbath. Think of it as a Bible Study Fellowship led by a successful businesswoman for her family and employees.

Second, there was a young woman possessed by a demon that enabled her to tell the future. She was not a total charlatan. She could actually tell the truth but in a way that was a huge distraction for Paul's work. After several days of her following Paul and crying out to people that he was here to tell people about how to be saved, he ruined her career and her owners' hopes of making money by driving the demon out of her (Acts 16:16–19).

Third, there is the jailer into whose care Paul and his friends are put after they are stripped and flogged for throwing the city into an uproar and threatening their customs and practices.

> When [the jailer] received these orders, he put them in the inner cell and fastened their feet in the stocks. About midnight Paul and Silas were praying and singing hymns to God, and the other prisoners were listening to them. Suddenly there was such a violent earthquake that the foundations of the prison were shaken. At once all the prison doors flew open, and everyone's chains came loose. The jailer woke up, and when he saw the prison doors open, he drew his sword and was about to kill himself because he thought the prisoners had escaped. But Paul shouted, "Don't harm yourself! We are all here!"
>
> The jailer called for lights, rushed in and fell trembling before Paul and Silas. He then brought them out and asked, "Sirs, what must I do to be saved?"
>
> They replied, "Believe in the Lord Jesus, and you will be saved—you and your household." (Acts 16:24–31)

Let's look at three things about this story.

1. There are two kinds of self-sacrifice. The jailer is prepared for suicide because he has failed miserably in his duty. Jails were not like we have today. They were a family business, and it's likely the jail was actually a part of his house. There was an assumption that failure came at the expense of your life—and perhaps even that of your entire household. The jailer's work was his whole life, and if he failed he might as well be dead.

There are many people for whom their work is their life, and failure is fatal. They cannot face the shame of it or the loss of social standing and esteem. There is nothing underneath to prop them up and they run away, self-destruct over time, or kill themselves. Failure in work or career means some kind of sacrifice is required.

There are two kinds of emptiness in Scripture and this is one of them—the emptying of people who are full of themselves and their own ambitions, now becoming worthless.

The other self-sacrifice is Paul's as he describes in Philippians 1:20–21: "I eagerly expect and hope that I will in no way be ashamed, but will have sufficient courage so that now as always Christ will be exalted in my body, whether by life or by death. For to me, to live is Christ and to die is gain." Paul had nothing to lose because his life was no longer his own. Whatever success or failure he experienced was in the hands of God.

In his letter to the Philippians Paul describes how Christ emptied himself by taking on the very nature of a servant. Jesus turned loose of who he had every right to be and made himself empty of the glory that was his. That is the emptiness of true humility. It is not worthlessness or self-degradation. It is self-sacrifice for something greater than life.

2. Paul and Silas were in the inner cell—the most secure part of the prison. I've often thought about how we have those same places in our own lives. There are things we lock away in the inner cell where it is hidden. But what do we do when that which is locked up so securely gets loose and the things we feared the most actually happen?

For some, it destroys them or their careers. The hidden past or the secret life suddenly emerges and wrecks them.

For others, it is not so much a personal internal earthquake, rather an external hurricane strikes us. It doesn't shatter our foundations, but it blows everything else away. It is just as destructive, but it can be a turning point.

We've heard many times what C. S. Lewis said in *The Problem of Pain*. "God whispers to us in our pleasures, speaks in our conscience, but shouts in our pain: it is His megaphone to rouse a deaf world."[20]

I believe the earthquake in Philippi was not to release Paul and Silas but to

---

20   C. S. Lewis, *The Problem of Pain* (1940; repr., New York: HarperCollins, 2001), 91.

shake the very foundations of the jailer's life. Paul was already free. It was the jailer himself who was in chains.

I think we have partly over-spiritualized the jailer's question—"What must I do to be saved?" He was not just asking a theological question but the most practical and urgent question in the world. *How can I live through this and not have to kill myself and my family?* But Paul answers the question below the obvious, the question that is deeply buried in the fear of all of us who are keeping something prisoner. *How can I be as free as you are?*

But it's not just the jailer who is saved, is it? It is God's plan to save him and his whole household. In Scripture, it is the family and the household that is the basic unit of society—not the individual. While we may not understand it, I think it's fair to ask the question, "Is God interested in saving as many as possible or as few?" The whole family was responsible for the prisoner, and the whole family was saved (Acts 16:34).

3. That first worship service in Philippi was diverse and close-knit. All of our strategies tell us that churches are made up of people who look alike—similar ethnicity and economic levels. Not here in Philippi. It's a small congregation of two households and an out-of-work fortune teller. It is interesting that the word for household—*oikos*—also means a circle of influence and relationships. Imagine the eclectic group Lydia and the jailer brought! That is why Paul loved them and why he said, "I thank my God every time I remember you" (Phil. 1:3). How could anyone do anything but marvel at the odds of that collection of differences creating a church that would, as Paul said, "become blameless and pure, 'children of God without fault in a warped and depraved generation.' Then you will shine like stars in the sky as you hold firmly to the word of life. And then I will be able to boast on the day of Christ that I did not run or labor in vain."

I know how he feels when I look around my Sunday school room each week. A motley crew. A quilt of different characters. A mixture of backgrounds and tastes. "Stars in the sky . . ."

29

THREE HARBORS

Text: Acts 27

Nothing ever seems to be easy in Paul's life. Every journey is punctuated by hardship, opposition, riots, persecution, and obstacles of all kinds. Such is the case with Paul's putting out to sea on his way to Rome as a prisoner. He had never expected the gospel to lead to a charmed life. In fact, he was more accustomed to hardship than he was to success. So, it should not have been a surprise for those traveling with him that they were likely to have trouble one way or the other.

Along the way to Rome we read in Acts 27 about three harbors:

1. Fair Havens (v. 8)

2. Phoenix (v. 12)

3. Malta (v. 39)

Fair Havens is a harbor from headwinds and weariness. A place to stop when you are making little progress.

Phoenix is a haven for an extended period of time—an entire season. It's more than weariness or slow progress. Paul and his companions were hoping to spend the entire winter there until conditions improved and allowed them to continue. It's not always the place we want to be since all of us would rather be on our way and not delayed. Phoenix is not like missing a flight or hitting traffic. It is a harbor for the times when life is interrupted for whole seasons or even years until our lives resume.

Malta is a harbor for recovering from catastrophe. It is shelter for the times we lose everything in life and need a fresh start.

As you can imagine, every harbor serves a different purpose. Fair Havens is full of encouragement. Phoenix is an easy place to get a room for an extended stay. Malta has a full-blown shipyard.

We are all in search of different harbors, but I want to focus on the first—Fair Havens.

You cannot help but notice the way Luke repeats the description of the difficulty they encounter. In verse 7 he says, "the wind did not let us stay on course." Again in verse 7 he says "we made slow headway for many days and had difficulty." In verse 8, "we moved along the coast with difficulty and came to a placed called Fair Havens."

All of us experience headwinds in our lives, times when we seem to be making little progress in our lives. It's not catastrophic or life threatening but a daily weariness of working just to keep up. It's when everything is hard. Everything is slow. Everything is unresolved. It's like being on hold.

Look at the other description in verse 8: "We moved along the coast." They sailed close to the shore. They are not even really sailing—just creeping along the coastline and not getting anywhere. Do either of these images—held back by a contrary wind or sailing close to the shore—describe times in your life?

What are some of the headwinds in life?

Work and Career
- A dead-end job where you are bored or stuck
- Workaholics who are constantly frustrated because they can never get everything done

- Large corporation environment with endless paperwork and constant delays waiting for approvals and permission.

Circumstances
- Unexpected expenses
- A child gets sick, a car won't start, the roof begins to leak
- We have plans and the sitter cancels.
- We hear "What's this from the IRS?" "The car is making a funny sound." "I meant to take care of that but forgot."

Relationships
- *Marriage.* How often have we wondered when the other person is going to change and make life so much easier?
- *Children.* How many of us thought we were never going to make it through adolescence?
- *Family.* Many are in the "sandwich" generation where the kids still need help and parents are increasingly dependent on them. Family dynamics don't always get easier as you get older.
- *Friends.* We lose them or they grow cold and distant. They move away or have other interests.

Personal
- Depression and moodiness are more prevalent.
- Our health becomes more of a concern and even limiting.
- We are anxious about the future and our ability to live with the volatility. A steady diet of the news is bound to have an effect on us.

Spiritual
- Our disciplines become lax and there is little wind in the sails.
- The easy answers don't seem to work anymore but we don't know why.
- We feel we should be further along than we are compared to others we read about or imagine.

These headwinds happen when we don't know our direction and our "instruments" are not working—when we've lost our confidence and our momentum.

What are the harbors in our lives?

The word "fair" or "beautiful" (Greek word is *kalos*) does not mean safe or photogenic beauty; it means fit perfectly for the task. It's the same word you use when asking for the right tool in doing a job. You are not asking for a good-looking tool—but for the right tool.

Fair Harbor is the right place to tie up at times. God has created havens and shelters for us all along the way when we are weary. Different harbors have different equipment. Fair Harbor is not for rebuilding our lives after a ship-wreck. It is for the times we feel we need to sail close to shore.

I can think of at least four Fair Havens for us:

1. There are *places* that are havens. The most obvious (or should be) is the church. This is where we come to be encouraged and to know we are not in this all by ourselves. We all have a particular place—the beach or the mountains or the desert—that give rest to our souls. For some, a haven may be a museum, an art gallery, a park, even a backyard. All of these are places that give us momentary rest from headwinds.

2. There are *times of rest* and we should take them. It is what Scripture calls Sabbath. A vacation or walking or short breaks in the routine allow us to tie up from battling the current and the winds.

3. There are *people* in our lives who are harbors. Someone who does not feel the need to fix your life or hold up flash cards of cheap encouragement, pat you on the back, and send you on your way.

4. There are particular *passages of Scripture* that are harbors we can carry around with us. We don't need commercials with unrealistic prom-ises but we do need encouragement.
   "Be still and know that I am God" (Ps. 46:10).
   "My soul will find rest in God alone" (Ps. 62:1).
   "Cast all your anxiety on him because he cares for you" (1 Pet. 5:7).

All of us need harbors where the weariness is lifted and we bear each other's burdens, build each other up, and help us to look forward to sailing in the deep water, far from the shore and the winds behind us.

30

ENVY IS GOOD?

Text: *Romans 9–11*

Sometimes we wonder why theology and doctrine are important. Can't we just skip to the life application parts? Isn't it enough to be saved and then live a decent life? We need to understand Romans 9–11 to see the answer to these questions and to trust the character of God and what it means when he makes a covenant.

In a sense, you could say that all of Romans prior to this has been in anticipating these next three chapters. Paul assures us that nothing can "separate us from the love of God that is in Christ Jesus our Lord" (Rom. 8:39). But what is the next thing in the same breath he says? "I could wish that I myself were cursed and cut off from Christ for the sake of my brothers, those of my own race, the people of Israel" (9:3–4). In other words, even as he speaks of the impossibility of being separated from the love of Christ, there is a great sadness and concern for his own people Israel.

Rick Warren's book *The Purpose Driven Life* begins with the phrase, "It's not about you," and that is exactly the way to start our glimpse at these chapters. Without that in the back of our minds we will never understand what Paul is saying here. These chapters are about God's eternal purposes that include us but are larger than us. We are on the bus, but we are not driving. I'm not even sure we are in the front seats.

For Paul, the issue is the fate of Israel. It probably would help if we understand Paul uses the word "Israel" in three different ways in these chapters:

1. First, Israel is the race to which he belongs. They are his kinsmen and
   his people.

2. Second, Israel is a term used for those who now follow by faith and
   not by the Law. They are both Gentile and Jew. They are the true children of Abraham and the offspring of Isaac. For believing Jews, they
   are a remnant. For Gentiles, they are those who have been grafted on
   to the root of Israel.

3. Finally, Israel is a term he uses to describe the nation of Israel in chapter 11. They are the Jewish children of the covenant and are loved on
   account of the patriarchs. God has hardened the hearts of these Israelites for a time and for a purpose, but they are not lost completely.
   We'll see how Paul works this out later.

In chapter 10:1–3 Paul writes, "Brothers and sister, my heart's desire and
prayer to God for the Israelites is that they may be saved. For I can testify
about them that they are zealous for God, but their zeal is not based on
knowledge. Since they did not know the righteousness that comes from God
and sought to establish their own, they did not submit to God's righteousness." In other words, it is not heinous sins that separates them from God.
Just the opposite. It is their vain attempts to be righteous on their own. It
is not their perversion as it was with the Gentiles, but their pride that separates them from God.

And his desire is that all the Israelites will be saved, not just a remnant. He
doesn't say, "Just save 20 percent of my family," does he? Just as important,
he is not thinking about individual redemption but the restoration of Israel
for its original purpose so that the people will be called back and restored
to their role as a kingdom of priests and a holy nation.

How will they be restored to their original purpose? Not by being right but
by being reconciled. Not by rules but by a relationship. Not by trying but
by trust. They will be restored in the same way as the Gentiles by calling on

the name of the Lord. And that, of course, is the stumbling block. They have substituted the way of Moses for the way of Abraham. What was meant as a guide has become an idol.

But God is not finished with his people. He has hardened them for the benefit of the Gentiles but not permanently. Because of their transgression, salvation has come to the Gentiles so that they may be grafted on to the original root. The Gentiles have not replaced the root. The great irony is the Jews have become a light to the nations even as they are in darkness themselves.

I have come to believe that Paul's primary mission was always to save and restore his own people. In spite of his history of rejection with them and his vows to go only to the Gentiles, he returns time and again to the synagogue only to be despised and ridiculed. But there comes a time in Corinth when he says, "Your blood be on your own heads! I am innocent of it. From now on I will go to the Gentiles" (Acts 18:6).

But I don't think it was that simple. He didn't really abandon them. Instead, I think he was given a brilliant strategy over time. He concentrated on the Gentiles to make the Jews envious. Look at Romans 11:13–14: "I am talking to you Gentiles. Inasmuch as I am the apostle to the Gentiles, I take pride in my ministry in the hope that I may somehow arouse my own people to envy and save some of them." It would be envy that would cause the Jews to listen and believe.

There is more to it. When the "full number of the Gentiles" was accomplished (v. 25), then the time of hardening and blindness would be over. In a sense, the focus on the Gentiles was a means to an end for him. The more Gentiles he could bring in, the closer we would be to the salvation of Israel. The Gentile church was not the new Israel. Only the Israel of the Jews could be that. Only together could they be the Church under the headship of Christ.

In a real sense, Paul was a missionary to the Gentiles in order to bring about the salvation of the Jews. All of Israel will be saved. God will not revoke his promise made to the patriarchs. Not just the remnant of a few and not just the Gentiles who by faith have become part of the inheritance of the promise made to Abraham, but ALL of God's chosen, special, holy, peculiar people will be saved and restored to their original purpose and given a new heart because they are still beloved for the sake of God's irrevocable promise to their fathers. God's promise to Abraham is secure, and Paul's mission will be accomplished. It's not about us, is it? It is about Israel. It is about the covenant. It is about a promise made to Abraham—and while we play a part in this drama, the central plot is God's chosen and peculiar people.

31

PROTECT AND PROVIDE

Text: Romans 13

One might think the subject of government to be a whole new topic for Paul, but it is not. It was not a new chapter when he wrote it. Chapters and verses were only added later in the fifteenth century, so there would have been no separation between 12:21 and 13:1—"Do not become overcome by evil, but overcome with good. Let everyone be subject to the governing authorities, for there is no authority except that which God as established." In fact, it is good to read 12:17 through 13:7 as a single passage because there is really no interruption between Paul's addressing how we are to deal with evil and the role of government and authorities. The governing authorities are one of God's ways of our living in peace and dealing with evil. Ordained government established by God is an agent of God's protecting us both from ourselves and from those who do wrong.

In fact, if you look at the several passages in 1 Timothy, 1 Peter, and Titus, there is a consistent theme: "Pray and be grateful for those in authority that we may live peaceful and quiet lives in all godliness and holiness." There were no qualifiers on that even though Roman authorities were harsh, over-bearing, and often cruel. This is why it is so ironic in the political debates that the candidates professing to be Christians are encouraged to do just the opposite by their campaigns as well as their supporters. It is more than ironic. It is sad. We reward them for behavior that is just the opposite of what Paul is teaching.

So, the first thing we see is that the true source of government is God. It is not an invention of man. Whether the authority is benevolent or cruel. Whether we are treated well or badly, the authorities over us and to which we submit are there by God's design, and to rebel against them is to rebel against what God has instituted. It does not mean that every feature of government is divinely instituted. It does not mean there is one particular form of government that is more ordained than another. It simply means that we need government and authority of some sort whether it is bad or good. The option is violence and anarchy.

Government's first responsibility is not to provide good things. It is not to shoulder the burden of making life more satisfying or easier. It is not a leadership position. Government is there to allow people to live in peace and not be fearful of those who would rob them of that. When government strays from that, it turns good intentions—even the best of intentions—into tyranny because it has overstepped its ordained limits and violated its mandate. By its very design government is incapable of doing anything more than what was intended—to be God's servant in protecting us from evil and violence.

That would not have been much of a concern to Paul or the early church. Whether the emperor was good or not was not a point of discussion. Christians were essentially powerless—even disinterested in such things. They had to learn to live with a hostile environment and as invisibly as possible. The early churches saw themselves as people in a lifeboat waiting to be rescued and not as people hoping to infiltrate and change the structures of the world.

Now, I don't want you to think that Paul is describing an institution whose sole authority comes from those who are governed. He could not have held to that. These are not Paul's words or the words of the apostles:

> Governments are instituted among Men, deriving their
> just powers from the consent of the governed.–That
> whenever any Form of Government becomes destructive
> of these ends, it is the Right of the People to alter or to
> abolish it, and to institute new Government, laying its

foundation on such principles and organizing its powers in such form, as to them shall seem most likely to effect their Safety and Happiness.[21]

Do you see the difference between that passage from the Declaration of Independence and Romans 13? What is the source of government authority in the Declaration? Government derives its powers from the consent of the governed. How is that different from Romans 13? Government derives its legitimate powers from God himself. In the one system we are citizens and the final authority, while in the other we are subjects and are required to submit to the authorities. This is very difficult for Americans and other democratic countries to swallow. It is especially difficult for societies like ours that were birthed with revolutionary values and whose founding fathers often spoke of the value of revolution whenever governments overstepped their bounds. For Paul, the rulers and magistrates did not protect individual or collective "rights" but were put in place to protect us from chaos and punish wrongdoers.

We have a different form of government, but its function in God's eyes is the same: to protect and not to provide. It is only when the prospect of chaos and insecurity is imminent that there is any reason for government to expand to meet the threat. Of course, that is how growth happens. The threat goes away but the increase doesn't. Fortunately, we have a means to change the government without revolution or rebellion. Civil disobedience, yes, but not outright rebellion and armed insurrection.

We should be grateful for the form of government we have. I regret that part of our legacy is a fundamental distrust and disdain for government and those who serve there. I am concerned that we now see the ultimate source of government not as ordained by God but created and accountable only to us. I have no interest in a Christian government as it would only become another form of tyranny in time, and I believe that the State has more to fear from the Church than the reverse.

---

21 https://billofrightsinstitute.org/primary-sources/declaration-of-independence

Finally, I would say that if we spent half the time praying, interceding, and giving thanks for those in authority that we give toward plotting against our partisan enemies, we might well have more of what we desire and less of what we deserve. Instead of focusing on controversy and disputes, it might be better, as Christians, to follow Paul's advice to Titus:

> Remind the people to be subject to rulers and authorities, to be obedient, to be ready to do whatever is good, to slander no one, to be peaceable and considerate, and always to be gentle toward everyone. . . . And I want you to stress these things, so that those who have trusted in God may be careful to devote themselves to doing what is good. These things are excellent and profitable for everyone. (Titus 3:3–8)

Let's devote ourselves to living in harmony and humility. I know that is not the way of the world, and it is likely not the way to win political battles and power. But Paul was not giving practical political advice, was he? He was telling how we are to live as citizens of another kingdom even while we are here in the world.

32

MY WEAKER BROTHER

Text: Romans 14

What does it mean to have weak faith?

It's not a bad thing. It doesn't mean "wrong faith" or someone who does not have saving faith. We have to remember that Paul makes a distinction about two kinds of faith—a distinction between *salvation by faith* alone and *growing in the faith*. In Romans 14 Paul is talking about one whose faith is new and undeveloped. In other words, there is a relationship between weak faith or immature faith. Martyn Lloyd-Jones says, ". . . the weaker brother is governed by the spirit of fear—that is why he multiplies rules and regulations. He is so anxious to hedge himself in, and to prevent himself from falling, that he gets to the point at which he is a legalist, falling back on justification by works, and denying justification by faith only."[22] They have accepted the gospel, but they have trouble being confident in the gospel and God's now being pleased with them through their trust in the complete work of Christ.

Weak in the faith describes those who have not yet come to confidence in Christ alone, so they need additional rules and regulations. It's not all bad . . . unless we never get past it. Everybody has to start somewhere. What

---

22   D. Martyn Lloyd-Jones, *Romans: An Exposition of Chapter 14:1–17 Liberty and Conscience* (Carlisle, PA: Banner of Truth, 2004).

are the fundamental habits in learning golf? Keep your head down. Firm stance. Right grip. Eventually, those things become ingrained and while they are still fundamental, they are not re-learned over and over again. The fundamentals allow us to move on and to experience the joy of what we are doing.

Paul describes all of these fundamentals when he tells us the Law was our tutor. The rules were necessary and useful when we were just learning how to behave, but now we have something far more powerful than a tutor. We have the Holy Spirit not only to instruct us but to provide the power to live this impossible life. Have you tried steering a car with power steering when the engine is off? It is far more difficult than manual steering, isn't it? That is a good description of the Christian life. We have not been designed for manual steering—and when the power goes off, living the Christian life is actually harder than the non-Christian life.

How is the church to respond? Paul says the church is to accept them (Rom. 14:1). Now, that word means something more than mere acceptance. It means to take into yourself in the same way you would absorb and digest food. Take them in completely and accept responsibility for them—not just include them as members to be counted. Incorporate them.

It does not mean put them into leadership or hold them up as examples of new faith if they happen to be celebrities. It means find a place for them to quietly grow.

Don't dumb down the church in order to attract people of weak faith. But don't try to indoctrinate them or force them into believing things that are really inconsequential. Instead, expect them to grow and not to stay weak in their faith. They may still hold to some of their rules of conscience but they will have a chance to examine them as they grow in their faith.

Paul often uses the phrase "I am convinced" (v. 14), and that is what he means here. Becoming fully convinced or confident is a process. Paul came to a belief over time that he finds no need to argue or be defensive about. That is the kind of environment the church can be in which people with widely different interpretations and preferences can be fully persuaded and not forced into a set of rigid opinions. The church is not a place of arguing, debates, name-calling, and win-at all-costs. In some ways, we in the church have contributed to the atmosphere of partisan strife and bitterness because we have made every difference we have with each other a battle instead of being a place where people have the freedom to become fully persuaded over time and in their own way.

We are not to sweep these things under the rug or to overlook sinful behavior. But we are to never stop working at unity, humility, and putting others interests in front of our own. Our goal is always the maturity of the church. Becoming fully persuaded is hard work and it takes time, teaching, and trust. People still want easy answers that do not require dependence on the Holy Spirit. We want policies instead of maturity. We want certainty instead of growth. Being confident in our freedom is not the same as being reactive or rebellious or throwing off our upbringing or demanding that others do the same. It means holding to things that really matter and that strengthen the body and turning loose of those that only cause problems.

There must be a mutual commitment and responsibility to move toward maturity. If we bend too far toward the "weaker brother or sister," we are only hindering his or her growth. If we give up things that are perfectly acceptable to our conscience, then we are being held hostage. Paul says we are to give up things that will truly cause another to fall or cause their deep hurt or their destruction—something that will directly cause them to fall back into sin (v. 13).

But the weaker one has an obligation to grow and not remain stubbornly weak. If they continue to control others by their own weakness, then they are not fulfilling their responsibility to become mature. Otherwise, the weaker brother or sister sets the standard and the stronger Christian becomes a caretaker. That is not love and that is not freedom.

What is the takeaway?

Advice to veteran believers: Don't judge or criticize those who are learning the ropes. Don't cause them to give up or quit by holding the standards too high or making fun of their progress. Commit to helping them stretch and see things differently without feeling they have to give up everything they believe. Don't offend them with your freedom, but don't let your freedom become your master. Don't lord it over them with your opinions or make them feel stupid. Play your own game without bragging or pride. Remember what it was like to be a rookie.

Advice to new believers: Don't condemn people as liberals who have worked their way through these issues and have freedoms you don't at this point. Learn from them as they learn from you. Don't be afraid of them or being seen with them. If you are unsure of yourself, ask those who have done the hard work of becoming confident in what they believe to be your mentor and find out what they have learned. But don't try to become who they are without going through what they have. Don't get out in front of yourself. Relax, practice, and grow. Be fully convinced.

"Let us therefore make every effort to do what leads to peace and to mutual edification" (Rom. 14:19).

33

AN INTERRUPTED LIFE

Text: Romans 15

Paul's letter to the church in Rome probably has had more impact on Western civilization and the life of the church than any other he wrote. His influence while imprisoned in Rome provided the foundation for the institution that filled the vacuum after the fall of the Roman Empire. St. Augustine was converted by reading it. Martin Luther was inspired by it to start the Reformation. The theology that allowed the eventual spread of the church beyond Judasim is defined here. In some ways, the concepts of natural law which led to the founding of this country are here. It's hard to imagine history without this one letter to the church at Rome. It's much more than a book in the Bible. It became the foundational document of an entire civilization.

We see in Romans 15, the final chapter, Paul's ambition is to preach the gospel where Christ is not known, so he plans, after visiting the church in Rome, to go on his way to Spain (Rom. 15:23–24). His role was always to proclaim the gospel but never be the long-term pastor of any church. He laid the foundation and then found those who could build on it. He found leaders and managers.

And now, with his work done and his task of raising the offering for the poor in Jerusalem almost complete (vv. 25–28), he is ready to go to Spain, but not before "passing through" Rome (v. 24). Paul always had plans and dreams, but they were subject to God's change. He was not a fatalist, thinking he had no choices. But he knew he served God who could change his plans and interrupt his life at will—sometimes for years. He never sat and waited for God's "perfect" will, but he knew everything somehow was worked together for God's will (Rom. 8:28).

We can always be headed toward our own "Spain" in our lives . . . but sometimes we pass through a time in Rome in ways we don't expect. Our dreams are interrupted or sent in a different direction and God offers no explanation. "I'm finished with my work here and I'm excited about my plans for the new work and I'll pass through quickly on my way."

What actually happens to Paul? He comes to Rome in chains and lives under house arrest for two years! (Acts 28:30–31). Yes, he gets there but not as planned and not just passing through. He is under house arrest and has just enough freedom to realize how constrained he is.

We all face the reality of Rome on the way to Spain, don't we? We have plans and dreams for our lives once we have finished with the tasks at hand. We have things we want to do once we have been freed of hindrances but then:

- A sick spouse
- Aging parents
- Children come home
- Finances change
- We have new and unexpected responsibilities
- Our health will not support our plans

We begin to realize, as did Paul, that our dreams and plans are always subject to change, and the issue for him—and us—is how to use the change. Do the changes derail us or only delay us? Do we resent them or realign our lives around them?

"For two whole years Paul stayed there in his own rented house and welcomed all who came to see him. Boldly and without hindrance he preached the kingdom of God and taught about the Lord Jesus Christ" (Acts 28:30). His purpose was not hindered by his circumstances.

But more than that, Paul's two-year imprisonment was a turning point in the history of the church and Western civilization. Roman law required a court trial within eighteen months. His failure to go to trial could mean that there was no case and this gave the Christian movement a quiet and unofficial legal approval. That would have allowed it during those two years to spread throughout Rome and the Empire until the persecutions of Nero.

In other words, we cannot know how God will use what we can only see as a prison or a hindrance. We cannot know what the power is of a single letter that survives against the odds. What we see as an inconvenience is God's intention.

And what about the dream of doing new work in Spain? Did he ever get there?

One church tradition says he was released after those two years and preached in Spain until he returned to Rome and to martyrdom by beheading. But what a life!

In 1903, a young, bright man named William Borden graduated from high school—a millionaire. He was the heir to the Borden Dairy fortune. Following graduation, William traveled around the world. Everywhere he went he was touched by the needs of people. He eventually wrote his parents to announce he would give up his fortune and devote his life to missionary service. In his Bible he wrote two words: NO RESERVES.

After enrolling in Yale in 1905, William quickly became the spiritual leader of the entire campus. He spearheaded a revival movement that led, by his graduation, to 1,000 of Yale's 1,300 students becoming involved in weekly Bible fellowships. He led off-campus, inner-city ministries as well.

Upon graduating from Yale, he repeated his intention to be a missionary and enrolled in seminary. Upon receiving his ministerial degree, he decided to take a one-way trip to Egypt where he would learn Arabic in order to reach Muslims with the gospel. Leaving all his fortune behind, he set sail. On the way he wrote two more words in his Bible: NO RETREATS.

He arrived in Egypt full of anticipation and immersed himself in the tasks at hand. But within days of his arrival, he became very weak and was soon diagnosed with spinal meningitis. A short time later, William Whiting Borden died at the age of twenty-five.[23]

Human logic can never understand his death, yet an ocean away hundreds were impacted because of his joyful, willing, sacrifice. That's the way William would have wanted it. During the last fleeting days of his life, in labored handwriting, he had penned two more words in his Bible: NO REGRETS.

No reserves. No retreats. No regrets.

"I have fought the good fight, I have finished the race, I have kept the faith" (2 Tim. 4:7).

---

23 Ronnie Floyd, "William Borden: A Life without Regret," *Outreach Magazine*, July 8, 2018, https://outreachmagazine.com/features/discipleship/31313-william-borden-life-without-regret.html.

34

TRUTH OR CONSEQUENCES

Text: 1 Corinthians 5

What do we do when we live in a culture that desires to redefine not only right and wrong but what is true and false? Are our personal choices *really* affecting the body of believers as a whole?

In 1 Corinthians 5:1–13, Paul is addressing not simply a particular sin—a man sleeping with his mother or stepmother—but the attitude of the church toward it. They are not only accepting of it but actually proud of their attitude toward it. They have no shame or guilt about the issue; it is something they consider to be a mark of distinction for their congregation.

They have taken some of the things Paul has said about freedom and twisted them to mean there are no rules. For example, in 1 Corinthians 6:12 he quotes himself as saying, "I have the right to do anything" but then has to go on to explain what that really means.

In Romans 3:21 Paul writes about righteousness "apart from the Law" and some in the early church took that to mean there were no laws and rules. They could do as they pleased with their bodies and their minds. In fact, one of the earliest heresies was about this very point. Gnosticism taught that our bodies were evil and our souls were good. Therefore, it did not matter what we did with our bodies because it was only our souls and minds that mattered.

It was a constant battle then—and now—for the church to decide what is legalism and what is proper order. What is law and what is license? This is why there seems to be a growing rift between our perception of Jesus and of Paul. Jesus was loving, accepting, and tolerant of sinners of all kinds, while Paul seems narrow-minded, opinionated, and harsh. It's a false choice.

There is another way of viewing this issue of choosing to sin. Look at Luke 17:20–21: "Once, on being asked by the Pharisees when the kingdom of God would come, Jesus replied, 'The coming of the kingdom of God is not something that can be observed, nor will people say, "Here it is," or "There it is," because the kingdom of God is in your midst.'"

When Paul says the wicked will not inherit the kingdom of God, we have often taken that to mean these people—thieves, drunkards, slanderers, swindlers, and greedy people among other kinds of sinners—will not go to heaven. If that is the case, then what hope do any of us have? Maybe another way to read this is, these people will not *experience* the kingdom of God *here in this life* as much as we might. Our sin separates us from our inheritance— but not condemning us to damnation. Perhaps we inherit as much of the kingdom of God as we choose in this life as well as in the next. The more we choose the kingdom in this life, the more we will enjoy the complete kingdom in the next.

We can redefine what is right and what is wrong, but we cannot redefine what is true and what is false. It was not only a particular kind of sin that was growing in the church at Corinth. It was the attitude toward sin that was infecting the rest of the church.

I say "infecting" because that is how some sins operate. Jesus told a parable of the wheat and the tares (Matt. 13:24–30). Tares are weeds that grow right alongside the good crop of wheat. Some divisions in the church are "wheat and tare" issues. If you try to resolve them completely, you will destroy the church. However, there are some life-and-death issues that attack the life of the church. What Paul is addressing in 1 Corinthians 5:6–8 is "leaven and yeast" that destroy trust in congregations and the entire fabric of a community. Paul is not simply addressing personal holiness here. He is fighting for the life of the church as a body.

Why is he so interested in immorality and sexual sin? Because the broken connection between immorality and our understanding of God and ourselves infected Israel over and over again. Look in Deuteronomy: "You must not worship the LORD God in their way. . . . be careful not to be ensnared by inquiring about their gods, saying, 'How do these nations serve their gods? We will do the same'" (12:4, 30).

Then Paul in 1 Corinthians 6 goes on to address how they are handling the everyday issues of disagreements and disputes. He is appalled they are so willing to set aside all moral rules but they are caught up in fighting over the trivial.

Once we leave the protection of right and wrong/true and false, we soon discover what happens. We turn on each other to protect ourselves from every slight and misunderstanding. We divide into camps and parties. We swallow a camel and choke on a gnat.

We lash out at each other in public and completely ignore the one great command Christ left: "You will love each other." The world looks forward to our next argument being played out in the media, which totally goes against how we should appear to an unbelieving world. They bait us with notoriety and influence, and we respond.

Finally, Paul is not just interested in personal piety. We are a body with obligations to each other. That word "obligation" is not very popular today. We see ourselves as independent agents who are free to move around as we wish. We have become "spiritual connoisseurs" who, like the Corinthians, have highly developed religious tastes and preferences but no commitments. Membership but nothing that would limit our freedom.

I think this is especially appealing to those of us who have the sense of "been there and done that and got the T-shirt" related to church. We've been on the committees, served as teachers, and done the mission trips. Now is our time to consider the church one of the many options for making our lives better. Our kids are raised. We have more time and outside interests. Why get tied down again?

But Paul is saying our lives are bound up with each other. My choices affect you, and your choices affect me. I like the way Dr. John English put it to me in talking about his view of leadership at Bethesda Clinic. He said his leadership responsibility was not just a personal responsibility of integrity but the responsibility of spiritual reality. His spiritual maturity matters to the organization.

Paul describes the things that dissolve trust and destroy community: greed, immorality, swindling, and theft. But what things weave trust as we practice them? Contentment, faithfulness, restraint, honesty, and generosity. When you choose them, you are making a gift to me. You are not just resisting personal temptation or growing spiritually personally. You are building up the church in ways you cannot see.

You and I will make choices today that affect each other tomorrow. When you choose faithfulness, it helps me be faithful. When I choose contentment, it influences you. When you are honest in your dealings with people, it builds all of us up. When I restrain myself, it makes a deposit into the general fund we are building up with our lives. That is how we grow together.

35

GOD'S FOOL

Text: 2 Corinthians 10–13

Bishop Michael Curry's sermon for the royal wedding of Prince Harry and Meghan Markle in 2018 was a beautiful example of a biblical view of love—not just romantic love. "We must discover the power of love, the redemptive power of love. And when we do that, we will make of this old world a new world. Love is the only way." As well, one of his most memorable lines was a reference to the love of Jesus: "Jesus did not get an honorary doctorate for dying. He wasn't getting anything out of it. He sacrificed his life for the good of others, for the well-being of the world, for us. That's what love is."

It is that unromantic and sacrificial love I want to focus on. The kind of love that keeps loving even when it is despised in return.

William Barclay calls 2 Corinthians 10–13 the "saddest and sorest and the most heartbroken chapters Paul ever wrote," and I agree. Instead of closing out with at the end of chapter 9—"Thanks be to God for his indescribable gift!"—Paul turns back to the rejection he feels from the Corinthians:

> By the humility and gentleness of Christ, I appeal to you—I, Paul, who am "timid" when face to face with you, but "bold" toward you when away! (2 Cor. 10:1)

It is certainly easier for me to be straightforward if I don't have to say it face to face. Judging from Twitter and Facebook, I would say many others are the same. We have less need to be pleasant and less reluctance to be honest if we don't have to see the reaction. People in Corinth felt Paul was the same way. Once he moved to another place (like Ephesus from which he is writing), he was tough on them and they saw that as a fault. Why couldn't he be articulate in person?

Paul responds to their charge that he is not as "Christian" as some of their other teachers who were claiming special knowledge that went far beyond Paul's simplistic understanding of the gospel. He says, "We have conducted ourselves in the world, and especially in our relations with you, with integrity and godly sincerity . . . relying not on worldly wisdom but God's grace. For we do not write you anything you cannot read or understand" (2 Cor. 1:12–13). For some, that was an insult. How dare Paul think they could not understand deeper things than he was telling them. How dare he question their intelligence or their maturity!

Paul's competitors in Corinth taught just the opposite. They told the people they were deep and deserved to move on from the simplicity of the cross. They deserved to have a fuller understanding and to possess the special knowledge that would make them intellectuals. The people dismissed Paul as too shallow. They were beyond him and, while they appreciated the simplicity of his message, they knew they were better served by more polished speakers and deeper thinkers.

I read an online article that reminded me of this passage and how I might have reacted to people who felt this way about me. It listed signs to watch for when it's time to move on from a relationship. Ask yourself if you think Paul had reason to move on:

- **When he/she is causing you emotional/physical/verbal hurt.**
  The wounds that are hardest to heal are the emotional ones, not the physical ones.
- **When the same situation/issue recurs even though you tried addressing it.**
  Do you keep landing in the same situation, the same outcome, no

matter what you do? If so, perhaps you need to accept this is the furthest the relationship can go.
- **When he/she puts little to no effort in the relationship.**
If you are constantly the one putting in more effort, sooner than later it'll drain you. Unless this imbalance is addressed, it will only become bigger and bigger over time.
- **When your fundamental values and beliefs are different.**
For any friendship or relationship to work out, there has to be certain similarity in fundamental values. If your core values are different, the journey to keep the relationship together will only become an uphill battle.
- **When you stay on, expecting things to get better.**
If the only thing that's making you hold on is the hope of a better future, the relationship isn't exactly built on solid ground.[24]

Instead, what does Paul do? This is the hardest part of this passage for me. In spite of their rudeness, ingratitude, disloyalty, and lack of love for him as their friend, teacher, and father in the faith, Paul not only stays but he makes a fool of himself to win them back. He almost begs them to take him seriously and keep their respect. He is knowingly humiliating himself so they will not abandon the gospel and fall for something else.

This is not the love we choose, is it? We want the feelings of mutual admiration or at least recognition of our love. This is not a picture of love we like to see. It makes us uncomfortable. We want leadership that is strong, and here what we see is pleading.

My response to this is, *Stop lowering yourself to try and prove your worth and your rights to their respect. They are not worth it. Have some pride.*

But he doesn't, does he? Instead, in spite of their treatment of him, he loves them. It reminds me so much of when God told Hosea to take the prostitute Gomer to be his wife. Even though Gomer leaves Hosea to return

---

24   Celestine Chua, "12 Signs It's Time to Move on from a Relationship," https://www.lifehack.org/articles/communication/12-signs-its-time-move-from-relationship.html.

to prostitution, God says to him, "Go show your love to your wife again, though she is loved by another man and is an adulteress. Love her as the LORD loves the Israelites, though they turn to other gods" (Hosea 3:1).

That was the heart of the people in Corinth. They had turned away from Paul's gospel and prostituted themselves with other beliefs and teachers. But then, the Lord says,

> "When Israel was a child, I loved him. . . . It was I who taught Ephraim to walk, taking them by the arms; but they did not realize it was I who healed them. I led them with cords of human kindness, with ties of love. To them I was like the one who lifts a little child to the cheek, and I bent down to feed them. . . . How can I give you up, Ephraim? How can I hand you over, Israel? . . . My heart is changed within me; all my compassion is aroused. I will not carry out my fierce anger, nor devastate Ephraim again. For I am God, and not a man—the Holy One among you." (Hosea 11:1–9)

That was Paul's response. He had every right to leave them in anger, but he wouldn't because he had taught them to walk, lifted them up, fed them, and led them with ties of love and cords of kindness. In spite of his disappointment and sadness, he would not abandon them.

That is Paul's glory and his pain. Perhaps it is ours as well in a relationship.

Paul closes with this: "We are glad whenever we are weak but you are strong; and our prayer is that you may be fully restored. This is why I write these things when I am absent, that when I come I may not have to be harsh in my use of authority—the authority the Lord gave me for building you up, not tearing you down. Finally, brothers and sisters, rejoice! Strive for full restoration, encourage one another, be of one mind, live in peace. And the God of love and peace will be with you" (2 Cor. 13:9–11).

That is redemptive love. That is the love of Christ.

36

HOLE IN THE WALL

Text: *Galatians 2*

Our focus on the book of Galatians actually gets its context from the early church in Antioch in Acts 11:19–26:

> Now those who had been scattered by the persecution that broke out when Stephen was killed traveled as far as Phoenicia, Cyprus and Antioch, spreading the word only among Jews. Some of them, however, men from Cyprus and Cyrene, went to Antioch and began to speak to Greeks also, telling them the good news about the Lord Jesus. The Lord's hand was with them, and a great number of people believed and turned to the Lord.
>
> News of this reached the church in Jerusalem, and they sent Barnabas to Antioch. When he arrived and saw what the grace of God had done, he was glad and encouraged them all to remain true to the Lord with all their hearts. He was a good man, full of the Holy Spirit and faith, and a great number of people were brought to the Lord.
>
> Then Barnabas went to Tarsus to look for Saul, and when he found him, he brought him to Antioch. So for a whole year Barnabas and Saul met with the church and taught great numbers of people. The disciples were called Christians first at Antioch.

Antioch was known for its cultural diversity and religious tolerance. Early believers knew they would be strangers but they would be safe. It was a city that attracted scattered people from all across the Empire and was able to absorb them.

But it absorbed them not by assimilation but by walling off the city internally. The city was divided into four quadrants with gates and walls. We have our own version of that even today. Cities are divided into sections that are bounded by streets—not walls. They are made up of high concentrations of particular races and cultures, and everyone knows where those boundaries are.

Shortly after arriving in Antioch, the Christian community had a remarkable distinctive. The believers lived in all four quadrants, but the church did not divide. It drew people from all four into one place. The church at Antioch had become a melting pot instead of a club or a neighborhood church—what we would call homogenous by attracting people who looked like themselves. The early church built gates and portals in the walls. They did not tear down the walls but they opened them to allow people to move from one quadrant to another and to join together instead of separately.

In fact, the church was so unique in this and crossed so many boundaries and mixed so many definitions and demographics that people had to find a new name for what they were. They were not Jewish or Gentile. They became known as Christians as there was no other description that could contain all the diversity they displayed.

I suspect it was Barnabas, one of the most respected leaders of the earliest church, who encouraged the diversity. After all, it was Barnabas who loved being with all kinds of people from many different places and saw the value of bringing a variety of cultures and backgrounds together.

And that is where our story begins: Galatians 2:11–15.

> When [Peter] came to Antioch, I opposed him to his face, because he stood condemned. For before certain men came from James, he used to eat with the Gentiles.

> But when they arrived, he began to draw back and sep-
> arate himself from the Gentiles because he was afraid
> of those who belonged to the circumcision group. The
> other Jews joined him in his hypocrisy, so that by their
> hypocrisy even Barnabas was led astray.
> When I saw that they were not acting in line with the
> truth of the gospel, I said to [Peter] in front of them all,
> "You are a Jew, yet you live like a Gentile and not like a
> Jew. How is it, then, that you force Gentiles to follow
> Jewish customs?
> We who are Jews by birth and not sinful Gentiles know
> that a person is not justified by the works of the law, but
> by faith in Jesus Christ. So we, too, have put our faith in
> Christ Jesus that we may be justified by faith in Christ
> and not by the works of the law, because by the works of
> the law no one will be justified.

The Jews from Jerusalem are anxious to keep the club limited to as few as possible. After all, if you let too many of "those kind of people" in, you dilute the purity of the group and risk losing your distinctiveness. They wanted to keep their traditions, rituals, and celebrations that let everyone know how special they were. They wanted to hold on to their privileges and their identity and to keep the new people at arm's length.

We are all members of the church of Antioch in some way. The pull of being with people our own kind is part of our nature, and over time the definition of "our own kind" becomes even more narrow. We want to hear our news from people like us. We want to live with people like us. We want to have our children marry people like us. We want the world to fit and subscribe to our narrow but long-held definitions of righteousness. We long for the old days and the old ways. We want to be the chosen, the special, the elite, and the standard by which everyone else is judged. It is only through the power of the Holy Spirit that we can find those gates in the walls. It does not mean we don't have confrontations and disagreements. It does not mean we disregard our deep differences.

But what it *does* mean is the one command Jesus left with us is more difficult than any of the 613 laws and regulations in Judaism.

"Love one another."

"But what about . . ." "But what if . . ." I so much wish Jesus had left a list of what to do in each circumstance, but he didn't. He left only the Holy Spirit, and without the Holy Spirit we have lost all of our ability to follow that one commandment. We cannot on our own love one another.

Jesus left only one description of our identity—not evangelical, conservative, progressive, orthodox, or fundamentalist. What is the one sign that we are followers? "Everyone will know that you are my disciples, if you love one another" (John 13:35). How many ways have we changed that single command and sign of identity in the eyes of the world? We have expanded that to include they will know we are followers by how we vote or where we stand on prayer in schools, Second Amendment, immigration, Supreme Court appointments, and civil unions.

This is why the world desperately needs the church to build holes and gates in the walls and to confront the hypocrisies of those of us who desire, like Barnabas and Peter, just to get along with everyone. It is why the definition of Christian cannot be political or even a religious affiliation. It is not limited to one quadrant. It can only be those who love one another against all odds and obstacles.

37

THAT MIDDLE PLACE

Text: Galatians 5

Two words serve as bookends for this chapter: *freedom* and *destruction*. In between those two words is the message of Paul to the Galatians. Embrace one and avoid the other. Reject one and suffer the consequences of the other. In between those two options is where we live and find ourselves in our times as a country and a world.

> It is for freedom that Christ has set us free. Stand firm,
> then, and do not let yourselves be burdened again by a
> yoke of slavery. (Gal. 5:1)

Paul is not talking here about political freedom or slavery, even though this verse has been misused to say that. He is not talking about economic freedom, freedom of speech, or even religious liberty. It is conflict with Jewish converts who wanted new believers to meet the requirements of a Jewish identity and to conform to the rules. Paul wanted to open up the borders and give everyone equal access to everything.

How did the Galatians see it? He was tearing down and giving away their identity to strangers. You can see why they wanted to silence him. They wanted the best of both worlds. They wanted the benefits of the new without giving up their special status in the Roman Empire. They were not required to serve in the military, their synagogues were classified as colleges and not places of worship, and they were not required to have the image of the Emperor on their coins. Having non-Jews as part of the church would have jeopardized those privileges for everyone.

We have been freed from the yoke of something we need to do to get God's love. As Dallas Willard says, "Grace is not opposed to effort. It is opposed to earning."[25] Paul would be the first to agree that we strive to become mature, but he would never say that we strive to become righteous in God's eyes. We need to lead disciplined lives in order to honor God, but obedience to rules is not the way to God's acceptance.

For many people brought up with the notion of a God always watching for someone to do something wrong, this is almost impossible to comprehend. We only have to accept the freely given love of God. For others, they need to be made free not only from their own self-judgment—the inner critic—but from their constant need to find fault with others.

We keep going back to our desire to satisfy God with a sacrifice, an offering, or a vow. Rules are both a whip and a reward—a carrot and a stick. They are real, and you know exactly where you stand. There is no ambiguity or uncertainty. When you obey them you are rewarded, and when you break them you are punished.

"For in Christ Jesus neither circumcision nor uncircumcision has any value. The only thing that counts is faith expressing itself through love" (Gal. 5:6). What does a free life even look like? How does faith express itself?

Faith does not express itself in the right ideology, correct economics, theology, patriotism, or party affiliations. It expresses itself in love for each other—no matter how we disagree. Is this suddenly easy? Can we be satisfied with tolerating each other? No, tolerance is not love. As G. K. Chesterton said, "Tolerance is the virtue of men without convictions."

---

25 Dallas Willard, *The Great Omission: Reclaiming Jesus's Essential Teachings on Discipleship* (New York: HarperOne, 2014), 61.

Human love, love for a child, love for country, love for a spouse, a parent, or dozens of other things is not what Paul means by love. That is a skill we can develop on our own with enough effort. We can take courses and seminars in that. What Paul is holding up here is "agape" or supernatural love that does not have its source in even the best of people. It is a gift from God, and no matter how hard we try we cannot manufacture it. It can only be received. There is no secret formula in the vault to preserve it.

One of the reasons we love runner Eric Liddell's quote so much—"When I run I feel God's pleasure"—is we do not feel it ourselves. Yes, we know God loves us and has forgiven us and we are somehow free from condemnation, but we do not feel his pleasure. We do not sense his joy in being with us. He has graciously refrained from giving us what we deserve, but wouldn't it be wonderful to truly *feel* God's pleasure? That is what Paul is saying here. In Christ, we can not only experience the justice, love, and forgiveness of God but also his pleasure. We can experience the "well done" in this life and not just in eternity.

But there is a purpose for freedom. We are made free from slavery to become willing servants to each other. There is nothing natural in this. It is supernatural. Everything in us makes us want power over circumstances, people, difficulty, and the unpredictable nature of life. But we are servants now—not free agents. It is not as free agents that we can love our enemies or those who persecute us. It is not as free agents that we can love those who insult, slander, and turn us into fools. That love is a supernatural act and a gift of God.

Why was Paul concerned about their abusing their freedom? He knew that the abuse of freedom and liberty would be the flip side of the coin. The rejection of freedom for rules would make them slaves again. Humanity cannot live with chaos. They would rather have tyranny. Paul was warning them that unless they understood that faith must express itself in love, they would eventually give up their freedom just to survive. Paul is calling the Galatians—and all of us—to live in that middle place where only wisdom and God's love can rule.

And that is where we meet the other bookend: *destruction*. Without the freedom that Christ brings, we will over time come to devour each other. When the church is no longer capable of supernatural love, then we are left in a world that can only do what it knows to do—fight for power, for prestige, for dominance, and the spoils of victory.

So, we really do live in the in-between, don't we? We are constantly tempted to give up the responsibility and ambiguity of freedom and always tempted to justify our desire to bite and devour those who disagree with us. Dallas Willard said it best for me: "The world can no longer be left to mere diplomats, politicians, and business leaders. They have done the best they could, no doubt. But this is an age for spiritual heroes—a time for men and women to be heroic in their faith and in spiritual character and power. The greatest danger to the Christian church today is that of pitching its message *too low*."[26] He is right. This is not a time for political or business leaders or even religious celebrities, but an age for spiritual heroes to find that in-between sweet spot, expressing their faith in love.

---

26 Dallas Willard, *The Spirit of the Disciplines: Understanding How God Changes Lives* (New York: HarperCollins, 1991), xii.

Parting Thought

Underneath the title of each chapter there has been the image of a scallop shell. That was intentional, as the scallop for at least 1,000 years has been the symbol of the pilgrimage of the Camino del Santiago that originates in France and stretches for almost 500 miles across northern Spain and ending at the Santiago de Compostela Cathedral. You will see the symbol of the scallop all across Europe on painted signs and even on tombs and monuments as far away as Ireland. The branched lines on the shell symbolize both the beginning and the end point of the journey. The variety of paths the pilgrims walk each day brings them closer together and closer to the final point of the journey.

That has been a metaphor for me in teaching. We have all begun from a different place on the outside of the shell but, hopefully, as we have walked together over time we have converged on the reason for our pilgrimage—the person of Jesus Christ. That is where I want to leave you now. I am grateful that you have been a part of this journey of forty years and, while none of us have fully arrived, we are all one day closer.

Made in the USA
Monee, IL
15 September 2021